The Magic of God's Love
The Love Theology of the Bible

John L. Tuff

To Dolores,
Thank you. I hope
this book will help you
to know the Magic of God's love,
May God richly bless you
Love
John Tuff

Xulon
PRESS

Dedicated with love to my wife, Patty,
and to Pastor Len Evans

To Len I owe not only a debt of gratitude but also a sincere
apology. His wonderful teachings have become so much
a part of me that I am certain I did not give him nearly
enough credit for ideas that now seem like my own.

The Magic of God's Love

In the heavens is a crowd of faithful witnesses
surrounding us like a cloud...

The cloud of witnesses was stunned. A pastor
was down...about to give up. His wife was leaving
him, his church pressuring him to resign. His hope
was gone. Belief in himself fading...This man who
knew at the age of sixteen he was to be a minister, who
at the age of twenty-two started a very successful Teen
Challenge Center in Rochester, New York, who had
pastored a community church for the past fourteen
years...The cloud of witnesses looked intently to see
what would happen next...

CHAPTER ONE

The Loving Creator

Growing Up in a Loving Community

L ife is magical! I believe with all my heart that God's desire for you and me is for us to live lives filled with Magic—the Magic of God's Love. Nothing else matches who *He* is.

What do I mean by magic? I mean the joy and exhilaration of a child on Christmas morning, the excitement of a date with that special someone, the pleasure of seeing happiness on the faces of your children, the serenity of watching a beautiful sunset in total peace, the joy of succeeding at something very important to you. It is the sense that life is special and that my life is very special. As an old hymn describes it: It is joy unspeakable and full of glory! I just call it Magic.

What I share in this book is the missing piece to the abundant life puzzle. How it got lost seems almost incomprehensible, since Jesus could not have made it clearer. When Jesus, the very agent of creation, summarizes all of His teaching into one final statement, it has got to be the key to the universe itself, and it is this:

A new commandment I give you, that you love and care for one another in the same way and to the same degree that I have loved and cared for you. (John 13:34, author's paraphrase)

Bruce Wilkerson writes powerfully about the life that God rewards. The *only* life God rewards is a life built on the love commandment.

Francis Schaeffer asked a very meaningful question: How should we then live? There is really only one answer: We have to live out the New Commandment.

Rick Warren has used his wonderful gift to get people thinking about a purpose-driven life; the ultimate and only legitimate purpose is to live out that love commandment.

Wonderful teaching, wonderful wisdom, but for me, the loop was not closed until I understood that Jesus wants from us only one thing: that we love one another.

Who am I to claim I found the puzzle piece? Well, the truth is that the only credit I get is that I was hungry enough to devour the truth when the Lord graciously brought it my way.

In fact, every day, as I begin my time of prayer with God, I thank Him for the love teaching of the Word and the very special mentor who shared it with me. (Thanks, Len).

If you are hungry, as I was, this look at the Scriptures will change your life, I promise! If you are satisfied with what you have, I doubt you will find a lot here—at least not now.

This is about three great discoveries:

- the wonder of who God is
- the wonder of who I am
- what God really wants from us (and why)

These discoveries were made not through great success but something of the opposite. I will share with you my personal journey of faith. I will be as honest as I dare. You will discover truth that can fill your life with the Magic of God's love.

In October of 1992, I spent two of the most productive hours of reflection I have ever experienced. I was in Orlando, Florida, for a conference on Career and Outplacement Counseling. I was attending with Deb Koen, my supervisor at Career Development Services, where I worked as a counselor for ten years.

On our final morning in Orlando, I went to Disney World to ride the Monorail and visit two of the hotel resorts where I had stayed on several vacations since the mid '70s. I wanted to spend this time all alone.

I stopped first at the large A-framed Contemporary Resort. As I walked around the lobby, went in to the game room, and walked around the beach area, I could vividly recall event after event with my children at each location, each pool, each stairwell. I could picture their joy and excitement during each visit.

Next, I went to the Polynesian Resort. I found an empty lounge chair at the edge of the beach and sat down to begin the reflection I had come to do. Once again, I just drank in the marvel of the resort, the beach, the view. Off to the right I was surprised at how close the Contemporary was, and then realized that was because I had looked so often at photographs in which it appeared to be farther away. I looked straight across and again had that incredible sensation that comes from seeing Cinderella's castle on the horizon of the lake before me. Once again I felt the incredible magic of this place.

I found myself talking to God, expressing heartfelt thanksgiving for all that had happened in my life during the past few years. It had not been easy, but I had so much for which to praise the Lord. I started, as always, with my beautiful and wonderful wife, Patty. She had given me a whole new life. Then, my children, Karen, Kathy, and Jason. Had I known some of what they were going to put me through in their teenage years, I might have left them at the Polynesian back in the '70s, but I was so thankful to God for the good things that had taken place in their lives.

Now it became a little more difficult, even painful, as I began to reflect on all of the dreams I had dreamed back then. Dreams of a life centered in God, dreams of a church ministry bringing joy and life to the people of my congregation, dreams that had been shattered by events both under and out of my control. Why had so many years been wasted? Why had so little been realized?

I continued to drink in the beautiful view and more of the beautiful memories. I began to sense the presence and love of God, and once again I was praying, praying that somehow, some way, I might recapture again the Magic I had felt back then in being so close and so loved.

I began to formulate some goals. I wanted to really live as a child who knew he was dearly loved by God. I wanted to find again the incredible Magic that I had felt at one point in my life many years ago. By Magic with a capital "M", I did not mean the magic of Disney World; I meant the Magic of knowing love and joy and peace in the Lord. There was a time when I found so much excitement in that that I could literally have jumped for joy.

It was time to head back. I walked back through the beautiful lobby of the Polynesian Resort and climbed aboard the monorail. And as it pulled out, I took one last look at that place, and I promised myself and God that I would find that Magic again and never let it go. And I did!

I believe that God is Love. It is not that He has love, not even that He has a great deal of love...He is Love. I think I have known that all of my life.

I never truly appreciated it, but I grew up in a very loving community. I am sure this has a great deal to do with my beliefs about God. My house was located in the middle of five mill houses that stood about thirty feet apart on a little country road in Mottville, New York. These five homes were originally built to house workers of the small mill that was located just down the road from us. After World War II they were sold off, and my parents were fortunate enough to purchase one for about eight hundred dollars.

In my growing-up years those houses were filled with some very special families. Right next door lived the Woodfords, Claude and Janie. They had three children. Harriette was about five years older than I, Ellen was about three years older, and Eddie was one year older. We were literally as close as brothers and sisters. At times, Ellen was my very best friend, and throughout Eddie and I shared the friendship and rivalries of real brothers.

On the other side lived Mr. and Mrs. Crane. It was like having built-in grandparents. Mrs. Crane was truly a loving grandmother to us kids. She was the one I wanted when I was sick. She was a beautiful, wonderful lady. When I had the humbling privilege of performing her funeral service several years ago, I realized that I had never, ever heard her say a negative word about another person. I had never heard her complain, even though her mobility was greatly hampered by having polio as a child. She put a lot of love into my life.

The remaining two homes housed younger families, the Reeds and the Pullens, with whom we also had wonderful relationships and good times. There were the usual squabbles, mostly among the kids, but it truly was like a loving extended family.

My parents, John and Ruth, were extremely loving to me and to my sister, Joan. They never made a lot of money, but they always made sure that we were provided for. I am clearly a child of the '50s. I was nurtured on Howdy Doody and the Mickey Mouse Club. I thought Annette Funicello was the most beautiful girl God had ever created. I loved Davy Crockett and Peter Pan. Then I discovered Elvis. I wanted to be the next Elvis, not only because I loved his music, but also because then Annette would be all over me! I really thought that families were like the Andersons on *Father Knows Best*. And, in many ways, my family was like that. I knew that kind of love, understanding, and security.

I think I always had a heart that was sensitive to God. I never really doubted His existence and always thought of Him as having the same kind of love that I was experiencing.

Every night when my parents put us to bed, we would say our prayers. Usually it was the "Now I lay me down to sleep" one. But in a way, I can trace my walk with God back to that ingrained habit. It never left me. Long after my parents had stopped putting me to bed, I never went to sleep without talking to God first. It helped to develop an enduring friendship.

Christmas was always a very exciting time for my younger sister, Joan, and me. Those were the occasions when I first experienced incredible Magic. Somehow, no matter what the finances might be like, my parents created tremendous joy and excitement.

Christmas Eve we would go to bed early, hoping it would make the morning come sooner. And each year we would awaken our parents earlier and earlier. Even years later, when I visited my parents, I could catch for a moment some of that same excitement as I remembered waiting at the top of the stairs those last few moments before it was time to see what Santa had brought.

But the Magic was more than just Santa and presents. I was also very much aware of the fact that we were celebrating the birth of God's Son, Jesus Christ. I could picture in my mind the events in that stable almost as if it were happening that very night. Even though I understood it in a very child-like way, it brought a great deal of joy and wonder to my heart. There was a Magic far beyond what the commercial Christmas could possibly produce.

One Christmas—I guess I was about eight years old—I got it into my head that I wanted to stop before we opened our presents and thank God for His Son, Jesus. Now, my family was not a strong churchgoing-type family. We went to Sunday school quite often, but that was about it. That, and those bedtime prayers, were the extent of formal activities. In order to be sure I would not forget to pray, I even hung up a sign that read "Don't Forget." That Christmas morning, for whatever reason, I was too embarrassed to bring it up. But that was my heart, that was my desire, that was how much even at that age I was sensitive to God. Often, in later years, God would remind me of that incident to show me that I was His and that my heart was not as hard as it sometimes began to feel.

As I moved on toward my teenage years I managed to convince my mother that going to Sunday school was pretty unnecessary, and so we stopped. My formal involvement with a church came to a close. My thoughts were filled with sports, rock 'n' roll, and girls. It was about this time that I saw the movie *A Summer Place*, starring Sandra Dee and Troy Donahue. It was all about the intensity and overcoming power of young love. I had suspected it because of Annette, but now I knew that the most important thing in life was finding love, finding the person created just for you. The god of Eros had won my heart completely. Nothing else mattered. Of course, it was still going to help a lot to be like Elvis so you would have a large number of girls to choose from as you looked for that one.

I now had a mission in life. And it was a very formidable mission, since I saw my chances of finding that girl as being very remote. I had large ears I had not yet grown into, and I was very skinny. I couldn't get a pretty girl to talk to me, let alone be the love of my life. Nevertheless, the god of Eros had created a hunger for my own Annette or Sandra Dee, and my mission was clear.

I continued to talk to God each night, but I was very concerned that He did not approve of the amount of time I spent thinking about sex. So I kept promising to stop, not understanding that at that age that is what boys do. Not knowing that, I felt there was now quite a chasm between God and me. I really felt guilty about it.

During these early teen years I spent a lot of time with Eddie, Ellen, and Joan. Then, Sally joined our group. She had moved from the village into the last house on our little country row. She was part of the "in group" at school, and she was a very pretty blonde. It did not take me long to realize there was no Eros in sight (although it made for great fantasies), and she became a real friend and a true member of our group.

We all were together constantly. We went to movies, played cards, listened to records, went swimming at the lake, and one night, we went to church together.

One Christmas when I was about fourteen, we decided to attend the Christmas Eve service at the Methodist church in Skaneateles. It was a crisp, clear evening as I walked into the church with Ellen, Eddie, Sally, and Joan. I was not expecting much to happen; we had just decided to go on a whim.

I do not remember much about the service itself, although I do recall a state police officer leaving early and in tears. What I do remember so clearly, what astounded me, was that as I walked into that church I sensed the unexplainable presence of a very dear friend: the One I had talked to each night. I was amazed to find the companion who listened to me in my room was present in this large and majestic sanctuary. The God of that church knew who I was! In fact, He was my friend.

Yes, I believe that God is Love. And I believe He knows each and every one of us intimately. The apostle Paul declared that it is in Him that we live and move and have our being. He is here, always has been, always will be.

What Magic! Think of it: a little boy would sit in his room each night and talk to the Creator of heaven and earth. God is that personal. And I believe He longs to be a part of our lives in that way. We can talk to Him any time, any place, and He is there.

And so, I believe that as a child I encountered the Creator and His Magic. I knew him as love; I knew that He knew and cared about me. I found Him because of my parents' love and the love I saw in significant others around me. I still had no idea how incredible and wonderful this person truly was, but I was on my way.

Have you encountered this person? If not, you can. He knows who you are.

O Lord, You have searched me and you know me.
(Psalm 139:1 NIV)

CHAPTER TWO

Loving Acceptance

Holy Cow! I Meet the Savior

It was the first time in my life that I had ever entreated God with a very specific request. I wanted a positive answer to my prayer.

I was fourteen years old and had begun to fill in as a Sunday school teacher. My Aunt Charlotte was the Sunday school superintendent of the Methodist church in Skaneateles Falls, New York. I was spending the weekend with her when she received a call from the preschool teacher. He would not be able to teach for the next two Sundays. At the time I was not even going to church, but I volunteered to teach the class.

I ended up teaching for several weeks. My aunt had finally given up on the first teacher and had arranged for a new teacher the following week. As I walked around that tiny church, waiting for my aunt to finish up, I suddenly realized that I did not want this to be my final Sunday. I wanted to continue to teach that class.

Even today, I still cannot explain why I wanted it so much. I guess the simple faith of those precious children was touching me. I can still remember some of them: Donna Lynne, Lietta, the twins, Mark and Mary; all were so trusting of what they were being taught about God.

I began to pray that week that God would let me keep teaching. I prayed hard. I told God that whoever that new lady was, I was sure she did not want the class as much as I did.

Somehow, I had a sense that God would answer. I just felt that it would work out. Maybe it was the first time I had prayed really believing that God would hear me.

On Wednesday evening of that week, my aunt called. She told me that the lady who was supposed to take the class had been stepped on by a cow, and the class was mine! Such was my early experience with answered prayer.

Due to that answer to prayer I became involved again in the church. Little did I know what God was going to do through all of this.

As I began to teach Sunday school I had the opportunity to get to know some of the other teachers. They were really wonderful people. I was the only teenager, and most of them had children in the Sunday school. One night, about six or seven of us were at Helen's house for a meeting. As the business part of the meeting wrapped up, we began to have an informal and wonderful discussion about faith.

Helen began it by sharing that she sometimes wondered about teaching the children things that she herself was not sure she believed. Others began to share some of their doubts and questions. It was a time of very honest sharing. I believed, I just felt, that God did not approve of my thought life (I was not about to share that since I still did not realize my teenage thought life was pretty normal). We had lots of questions, not many answers. In just a few months, most of this same group would come to know the reality of God in their lives and have unshakable faith in Jesus Christ!

In the summer before my senior year in high school a new minister came to the church. His name was Dan Benedict; he and his wife, "Mary O," were twenty-one years old. He was attending Syracuse University as well as pastoring our church. He had made a commitment of his life to the Lord while attending a small college in Kansas and had soon felt a call to the ministry.

They had a tremendous impact on the life of our little church. Actually, it was a two-church charge, one in Mottville and one in Skaneateles Falls. Until their arrival, there had been no youth activities. They started a youth group that soon drew close to thirty teens from the two communities.

The biggest impact, however, was what Dan was preaching. We were not used to someone who seemed to know exactly what it meant to be a Christian. We thought we should all try to be Christians, but how could you ever be sure? This tied right in to my struggle. I wanted God in my life, but I knew for sure that I was not good enough to be a Christian, to know that I would go to heaven.

I marvel as I look back at how God works. He touched the life of a young man reared in central New York who was attending college in Kansas. He sends that same young man back to New York to answer the struggles of a young teenager who felt he would never be good enough to please God. That is only a tiny part of what God accomplished through Dan, but it was, of course, vital to me.

Soon I was active in the youth group as well as being a Sunday school teacher. I enjoyed what I was doing but still felt I kept failing to be what God expected me to be. No matter how hard I tried, I simply felt that I did not measure up.

I was preparing to join the church on Easter Sunday of my senior year in high school. On Good Friday Dan invited me over to his study. He shared with me what he himself had discovered just the previous year.

He talked to me about God's love and God's grace. He explained that I did not have to, nor could I, earn my way into the family of God. I could, however, enter that family by faith. God would give it to me as a free gift.

He showed me where it says in the New Testament that those who will open their hearts and lives up to Jesus and receive Him are then given the privilege of becoming the children of God (see John 1:12).

I prayed with Dan that morning of Good Friday, and my life was changed forever. A huge burden was lifted, and I knew God's love and forgiveness. I was a child of God not because I had earned it but because God gave it to me as a gift through His Son.

My ongoing friendship with God now took on a whole new dimension. Jesus had become much more real to me. I did not suddenly begin to measure up, but I now began to experience the Lord's forgiveness and support.

The god of Eros had been put into second place—for now. There was no need to get rid of him; after all, finding true love is a marvelous goal. I had no way of suspecting at that age that this god would one day leap back into first place and almost destroy me.

Previous to this, I had already felt that I should go into the ministry. I now began to make concrete plans to move in that direction. As they say, if I knew then what I know now.... but, oh well, I didn't and headed eagerly down that road.

The next two years were wonderful growing years for me. I attended Auburn Community College and remained very active in the church. I had the opportunity to preach not only in our church but in several other area churches, as other ministers learned of my availability. On one occasion I even performed a funeral service under the guidance of a minister who had laryngitis. I was only seventeen at the time.

I had the joy of sharing my faith with other young people. I served as a camp counselor for two summers at

Casowasco, the Methodist youth camp in the Finger Lakes area of New York State. Many of my friends were making a similar commitment to Christ.

By that time, our little neighborhood group had pretty much broken up. My sister was engaged to the love of her life, Eddie was spending time with a new group, Ellen was working, and Sally was moving on with her life. I was now spending most of my time with kids from the church youth group.

I was surprised to realize that other teens were also concerned about their relationship to God. Like me, they had not known that you could actually be sure of God's grace and forgiveness. We had been raised in churches where the social gospel was being proclaimed. Doing good works was emphasized rather than a personal relationship to God. I found as I shared my faith with kids from other churches that this was all new to them.

Pam and Sue were campers the first summer I was at Casowasco. They expressed real concern about their standing with God. Pam was quite sure she would never be good enough. I shared with them what I had discovered about God's grace and how being a Christian is not based on our efforts but on our willingness to accept Christ and His forgiveness. They both prayed to invite Jesus into their lives that very night.

I am so grateful to Dan and Mary O. for the amount of time they invested in me and the other young people. Mary O. was a true mentor and disciple. As she freely shared her own walk with the Lord, her own prayer life, her own struggles in key life decisions, I learned much about walking with God. And Dan was a marvelous example of a young and committed Christian. (Of course, now I realize just how young they were.)

Through them, I met one of the most significant people in my Christian walk—Ernest Johnson. Ernest was a black man in his late sixties who spent his life going from church to church singing gospel songs of worship. He would come to our church about twice a year. When he sang, you were not watching a performance. You were simply watching a man of God sing to his Lord—you experienced a very special relationship.

But singing was not his true ministry—prayer was. He would pray about eight hours a day, praying for just about everyone he had ever met. From him I learned the importance and beauty of that kind of communion with God. I never got up to eight hours a day, but prayer has been extremely important to me, and Ernest instilled that in me.

During this same time I was also enjoying wonderful relationships with other adults of the church. I was part of a weekly Bible study and formed tremendous friendships with many church people, including Nina, who became almost like a second mother to me.

My hopes for Eros had been raised quite a lot during this period. There were a few girls that would not only talk to me but actually make out with me! One of them was quite pretty and very fickle. Of course, now there was a whole new wrinkle. I was now being taught that I had to find the woman who was God's choice, especially if I was going to be a minister. But what if God didn't choose Sandra Dee? Also, I had learned to play the guitar. I had a pretty good voice and had been singing at school functions since third grade. The catch was that I learned from a guy who knew mostly country western bar songs. So later, during my time of playing at Youth for Christ retreats and parties, my repertoire proved to be a little different than most. I doubt that "Chug-A-Lug" was a highly requested tune at other YFC locations. But, I got pretty good at playing, and it was true—the girls liked it.

Although I had opportunities to share my faith in various churches, youth groups, retreats, and camps, none of that prepared me for the tremendous anxiety I experienced on one particular occasion. I was sitting in my bedroom one night when I began to feel that God was telling me that it was time to ask my father about his relationship with the Lord. I vigorously pushed those thoughts aside for over an hour, but they just kept coming back.

Finally, I went into my parents' bedroom. My father had just gone to bed, and my mother had evidently fallen asleep downstairs on the couch. With a pounding heart, I talked to him about the free gift of God's love and forgiveness in Christ. This was not easy. "Poppo," as he affectionately became known through the years by his grandchildren, was a very private person—wonderful, but private. He just did not talk a great deal. I did not know how he would respond. He was a machine operator in a diesel engine plant. Men of that type simply did not seem to talk about those kinds of things. But that night, we prayed together, and he invited Christ into his life. I told him that this was the hardest "sermon" I had ever given.

My mother had already reaffirmed her commitment to God, and we now became much more involved in the life of the church. A growing faith, growing friendships, and a tremendous sense of God's love, guidance, and care...

As the years have gone by, over and over again I have thanked God for the very simple message of salvation. As a minister, as a counselor, as a friend I have continually encountered people who, like me, knew that they just did not measure up to God's standards or their own. What a joy to be able to tell them about the free gift of God's forgiveness and acceptance.

To know God as the Creator was very special. To know Jesus as my Savior gave me the joy of knowing the love and acceptance and forgiveness of my God. Whatever we have done, however we may have failed, the forgiveness of God is there for each and every one of us.

And now I knew that I truly was a part of His family—not because I was good enough, but because He loves me that much! It really is like magic.

As my journey continued, God confirmed for me in many ways that He is Love. One of the most compelling of these was my experience as the director of the Teen Challenge Center in Rochester, New York.

CHAPTER THREE

A Magic House

I See the Power of God's Love

From what you know of my life you probably wonder how I ended up living in the inner city of Rochester, directing a live-in center for those addicted to drugs and alcohol. It is all part of the path I followed after that cow thing.

I went to Roberts Wesleyan College near Rochester to begin my studies for the ministry. My plan was to get my B.A. there and then go on to Asbury Theological Seminary, which was where all evangelical Methodists were supposed to go. (At least that is what I was told.)

I wanted others who might be growing up in churches where they did not learn about a personal faith in Christ to have the opportunity to discover what I had learned through Dan and Mary O's ministry.

This was not a common message in the Methodist churches of Central New York back then. In fact, on several occasions, I was mildly pressured by other ministers to see that what Dan had shared with me was fine for Baptists but not for modern Methodists. But I knew what I had discovered was true. I had struggled a long time trying to be good enough. And I sincerely believed that the Bible was the Word of God. I was never impressed with those who tried to take it apart. I knew what a personal faith in Christ had done for our church and strongly believed it was needed elsewhere.

The summer before I started at Roberts Wesleyan I counseled at Camp Casowasco for a week. This was the second summer I had spent a week with Jack Buskey, one of the few area Methodist ministers who shared a faith similar to mine.

One of the other counselors was a young woman named Mary Jane. She was the secretary for the Methodist bishop in the area. She was very hungry to know more of God in her life. We would get up early and meet by the lake to talk about our beliefs and ideas about God.

Later in the summer Mary Jane sent me a copy of a book that meant a great deal to her. It was *The Cross and the Switchblade* by David Wilkerson. I had heard a lot about the book but had not yet read it. I devoured that book in less than two days.

It is the story of how a young minister in rural Pennsylvania is directed by God to go to the worst streets of New York City and tell gang members about God's love. Later, Wilkerson established the Teen Challenge Center, which ministered primarily to young people addicted to drugs. It is a very compelling story of how the power of God changed the lives of these young people.

I had learned much about a close, personal relationship with God, but this was the first time I had ever encountered such power from God in the lives of men and women. I was always hungry for God, so now it crossed my mind that perhaps there was something more available to Christians through the Holy Spirit. Could there be even more Magic?

A few weeks after settling in at RWC I met some students who believed very strongly in the work of the Holy Spirit as described in David Wilkerson's book. They too believed that the time of miracles was not over and that we could be filled with the kind of power one reads about in the book of Acts.

In essence, they were saying to me, "Well, John, it's great that you have received Jesus as your Savior, but if you really want to know God, then you need to be filled with the Holy Spirit."

For me, when God answered that prayer, it was a feeling more of love than power. It just brought more of that same person into my life. It was beautiful, but it did not suddenly make me a combination of St. Peter and St. Paul. There was, however, a greater sensitivity to God's love and God's guidance.

One afternoon, several of us, including my roommate, Bill Rushik, were sitting in our room talking about the needs of youngsters we were working with in the inner city of Rochester. We had been running some clubs for teens through the work of Rochester Youth for Christ.

We started "dreaming." We agreed with what one person said, "What we really need is to do more than just go down there once a week; we need a big house there so the kids will have a place they can come to any time—a center for them."

"Yeah," someone added, "and John, since you will be graduating in June, you can be the director."

We all laughed about that, because of course I was on my way to seminary to be a Methodist minister. The more we talked, however, the better it sounded. And we wondered if maybe God was in this. So, we prayed a naive but effective prayer.

"God, if this is not just our crazy idea, if You're in this, then let there be a house for sale right in the middle of the three blocks where we have been working."

Literally hundreds of lives would be changed. We contacted a real estate agent, and there was in fact a perfect house for sale right in the middle of that area. Still not convinced, I was in a prayer meeting that next weekend, and someone who knew absolutely nothing about this spoke in prayer about God giving success in the new venture that some in the room were considering. But we were still a handful of college students with no way to raise the eight-thousand dollar down payment it would take. Then, through another student, we learned that a group of ministers was trying to get a Teen Challenge Center started in Rochester. What they wanted to do looked just like what God had been leading us to do. I was selected to be the director, and a few months later, David Wilkerson came to speak at a meeting — and the eight-thousand dollars was raised that very night. Magic!

Even as I entered into a very powerful ministry of the Holy Spirit, I still was focused primarily on God's love. I remember even while being interviewed for the position of director this focus on love came through. I fielded questions from about a dozen ministers and other church leaders, and they wanted to be sure that I really had the Holy Spirit in my life. I shared my experience with them and also pointed out that I was convinced that the strongest evidence of a Spirit-filled life was love.

I started as director of the center in November of 1968. I was twenty-two years old, had been married less than four months to a young woman named Sharon whom I had met at RWC, and knew with all my heart that God had placed me in this ministry.

I first met Sharon at the orientation for new students the summer I transferred to RWC. I did not then think of dating her, although she did bear a striking resemblance to someone named Annette. I got to know her through various school activities and small group meetings. On our first date we went to church together. (What else?)

I began to court her. At least, that was my perspective. Her perspective is that I began to pressure her into a relationship without giving her enough space to decide. I convinced myself that she was the one. (Why *wouldn't* God give me someone who looked like Annette?) She was reared in a Christian home, played the piano, and would be a fine wife for any minister.

In that sort of Christian setting, it's hard to argue with someone telling you about God's will. I was trying to be sincere, trying to find out what God wanted, but the fact is I may not have been willing to hear God say anything else. To this day, I am not sure. And years later we would learn through counseling that making her own decisions was not Sharon's strong suit.

So, spurred on by the excitement of Teen Challenge and my sense of God's leading, we were married the summer after I graduated.

We were at Teen Challenge for three wonderful years, and during that time I saw the love of God at work in the lives of people who otherwise would have had no hope.

We started by continuing our work with young teens in the neighborhood. We were able to become a greater part of their lives now that we were actually living there and available on a daily basis. Bill Rushik was a huge help. He had one more year at RWC and would come in several times a week to work with the kids. He also recruited several other volunteers from the college to work with us. Sharon coordinated a Saturday program with little children from the neighborhood.

The highlight of the week was the Friday night chapel service, when as many as twenty kids would gather in the house to sing and hear about the love God had for them. Many tried to follow Him in their daily lives. What a joy it was to watch their growth despite the extremely difficult circumstances in which many of them lived.

Next, we started to go out on the streets and tell older teens about God's love. More and more often we began to run into those with drug problems. We had not intended to become a live-in center like Teen Challenge centers in other cities, but as the months went by, some of those with severe drug addictions showed up at our door wanting the help from Jesus that we had talked about. The center became a live-in program, and I was on call twenty-four hours a day. Most of the people we worked with were addicted to heroin.

It is one thing to talk in theory about what Jesus can do for someone. It is quite another to have people come to you who have tried program after program and tell you that this is their last hope. I found myself telling them that indeed Christ would help them, knowing that if He did not we were all in big trouble. Time and time again He did. So many young men come to mind who found new life in Christ.

Danny and Guy would later become a part of the church where I pastored. I would have the joy of performing their wedding ceremonies, as God gave each of them wonderful Christian wives, and then also watch their children grow up in the church. Walt, a young man from Boston who would struggle for years with his faith and ended up living with us in the church parsonage later during a time of need; Sonny and Mike—and Angel, who would later go to RWC and then into the ministry. Ricky, who drifted off on his own and then showed up as a TV and movie star, including a significant role in the movie *Ghost*; life after life, story after story.

And then there was the miracle of the center itself, on Alexander Street. Picture a large house filled with ten to twelve addicts, a couple of former addicts on staff, and an inexperienced minister from Mottville...and then realize that the house is filled with an incredible sense of family and care for one another. I was part of a miracle where the love of God was changing lives on a daily basis.

If there was such a thing as a typical day at Teen Challenge, it would start by getting the guys up for chores before breakfast. They were responsible for all the housekeeping.

Next, they would attend a chapel service led by me or one of the other staff members (usually someone who had been through what they were going through). Later in the morning there would be a class on Christian living.

In the afternoon, a staff member and one or two of the guys who were doing well would go to a local high school and present an assembly program. I might take another staff member and go to one of the areas in the city where addicts were hanging out to tell them about God's love.

The more we visited these places, the more these young people came to know us. Some days, we were the only people they could talk to who were not trying to rip them off. Once in a while one of them would decide to come back to the center.

Back at the center, a staff person would begin to help the new person settle in. The group would be back from the high school talking about how open the students had been to the message of God's power to change lives. They were often more skeptical about the warnings concerning drugs.

That evening there would be a time of singing and sharing in the chapel. A group from a local church might join us, bringing much-needed groceries. Someone would be upstairs praying with the new person who was beginning to kick his habit.

If it was summer, the evening might also include a trip to a local park; in winter, a chance to use a nearby church gym. And Jesus Christ was very much in the midst of it all.

At that time, the cure rate for those addicted to heroin was less than 5 percent. The cure rate for those who complete the Teen Challenge program has consistently been more than 75 percent. "Cure" is, of course, the wrong word. It was a miracle of God's love as these people came into a life-changing relationship with Jesus Christ. The federal government would often do studies of Teen Challenge trying to figure out the "cure." As far as I know, they still have not figured it out.

I always spent a lot of time in prayer. (Who wouldn't in such a setting?) One night I was alone praying in the living room, asking God to continue to help us meet the spiritual and physical needs of people in the center. At that point I had an experience that is hard to explain. I felt as if I were literally being immersed into liquid love. I "felt" love, and felt loved, as never before.

It was both a physical sensation and an intellectual assurance and awareness. *God is Love.* This was so much more than the friend in my room. This was His heart. This was His very core. Any doubt I might have had regarding that love was completely gone. I did not see God; I felt God with every fiber of my being. It was all love. I do not get many vision-type experiences, but this was one I would never forget. (Well, almost never, but that's for later.) At the same time, I was so concerned about how few people seem to realize that this incredible love is who God really is. And even as I was overjoyed in those moments with what I was experiencing, I asked God to help me help others to come to know that love. It was for me a whole new level of knowing that God is Love. And God would answer my prayer, though not on the path I had expected. I did not know that I would soon be leaving Teen Challenge.

The house was overflowing, but we were able to purchase a second large house right next door. We have no idea where the money for that house came from. Through our newsletter and a radio program on the Christian Broadcasting Network we had let people know of our desire to purchase a second house. In the mail came an anonymous donation that provided the money for the down payment.

Speaking of radio, that was an extremely exciting time for me, the child of the '50s who thought TV and radio were everything. On four occasions I appeared on the *Eddie Meath Show*, a local TV talk show. I was a little bit of a celebrity. OK, so I wasn't singing rock 'n' roll, but I was on the tube.

I even got to do a show with Erik Estrada to plug the movie *The Cross and the Switchblade*. At the time, that was something for a very shy kid from Mottville.

In fact, the ministry of Teen Challenge had produced a great deal of recognition. I would not be at all honest if I did not admit that it was very gratifying to be seen by many as doing a great work for God. But during those three years what I would see as perhaps my moment of greatest obedience in service to God took place far from the streets of Rochester— took place, in fact, on a dirt road back in Mottville.

My Uncle Claude was dying of cancer. Death was imminent. I had somehow summoned enough courage to go and talk to him. I was very nervous as I walked into his small house. He was lying on a bed in the tiny living room looking pale but very alert. The truth is that as a small child I was very afraid of him. I did not know him very well.

The most time I had ever spent with him was when I had driven him to a clinic in Buffalo a few summers before. My Aunt Gladys quickly excused herself, and I was left alone with Uncle Claude. The last time I had been in this room was a few years earlier when their son had been killed in a hunting accident. We never found out who shot him, presumably by mistake, and then fled. Claude, who had already been diagnosed with cancer, understandably questioned why God had not taken him instead of his young son. Now, I somehow wanted to share the love of that same God.

It took me a while to get started, but I finally began to discuss with him what he assumed I had come to share. Most of my family was still startled by the fact that we had a minister in the family. I talked about Christ's love and offer of forgiveness and the assurance Jesus gave us of eternity with Him. He was very open when I asked about prayer, and he followed my lead in asking God's forgiveness and inviting Jesus to enter his life as Savior and Lord. I told him of Jesus' assurance that He went to prepare a place for us and would receive us when we went to eternity. It may have been one of my few moments of true service. I overcame fear and did it out of obedience, not to be seen by men.

When I left I was not sure what he really thought or understood. Perhaps he had just been polite. Then, a few days later, his wife overheard the end of his conversation with a visiting friend. In parting the friend said, "Well, I'll see you again soon." My Uncle Claude answered, "If you don't, I'll be in a place better than anything you've ever seen." I'm pretty sure he is.

How I was blessed to see the Magic of God's love in those days; people being set free, groceries arriving while we were literally praying in the chapel about our needs for the next meal, and my own faith being strengthened each day.

At the end of the second year our first daughter, Karen, was born. The night of Karen's birth, October 4, 1970, was far and away the most outstanding night of my life to that point. I just had no idea how much love can fill your heart for someone who did not "exist" a moment ago. The joy, the wonder, the humble thanksgiving as I looked at that little child was as great an experience as the night earlier that year when I encountered God's love. Of course, it was the same source, same love. I suddenly knew something of God's love for His children that had been beyond my comprehension the day before. I even felt that I now understood a little more of the love and patience and unconditional support I had from my parents. So that's how they did that! (And that joy would be repeated with the coming of Kathy and Jason.)

We were thrilled; everything was going well. Not only did we have the live-in program, we were also being invited to countless high schools to share the stories of the people with whom we were working. We were not allowed to mention Jesus in our presentation but could freely answer when the students asked our guys what changed their lives. More than once, their simple expression of faith in the Lord Jesus was greeted by thunderous applause.

This was also the hippie era, and some nights as many as thirty or forty hippies would be seated in one of the large living rooms to talk about God and their lives. People would walk into the center and somehow sense that God was there—Magic!

As time went on, however, I had a growing sense that I was being pressured into being something that was not quite me. I had had a wonderful experience with the Holy Spirit, I knew the power of God in my life, but I was not a typical Pentecostal minister. As I said, even in my interview for the position, I had stressed that I saw love as the key rather than the powerful works of the Holy Spirit.

This even caused some problems for some of the guys in the program. After spending six to eight months with us in the Rochester center, they would be sent to the Teen Challenge Training Center in Rehrersburg, Pennsylvania. There, they were in a school and vocational setting with a hundred others from various centers in the Northeast. The emphasis was on discipline, which it needed to be.

The emphasis in our center, however, had been very much on love, that which I knew of God. There was a true and wonderful sense of family. A few of the guys found the transition to be very difficult. Some of the staff there were appalled that our guys did not seem to know that long hair was a sin. I had more than one discussion with the staff about my approach to this ministry. It would not be the last time that my awareness of the wonderful, unconditional love of God would be seen as a problem to those in authority.

Also, I am not a sales and marketing type, and some on the board felt that the director should be doing more in that area. Teen Challenge was financed totally through the donations of churches and individuals. I just thought that if we worked hard at ministering to the young people, God would provide the funds (which He consistently had).

I finally started to feel more and more pressure in these areas and prayed about leaving. Over a period of months, God opened a door, and I became the pastor of what was then Ridgeland Baptist Church, located just south of Rochester.

I had now seen the power of God's love. I had seen a true sense of family and community transform the lives of people the world had given up on. I had also seen the problems some Christians had with a concept of God's love that to them seemed too simple, too accepting.

But I knew Him as that! I saw what He had done for those young people I loved so much. And that night, I had spent time with Him, with that very love as real, more real, than any human encounter.

CHAPTER FOUR

A Magic Key

I Find Out What God Wants

I wanted so much to be what God wanted me to be. Dan and Mary O. had told me about the importance of receiving Jesus into my life, and I did. At RWC they seemed to say that it was great that I was "saved," but if I really wanted to serve God I had to totally commit myself to Him and get sanctified, so I did. Then, some others at RWC said it was great that I was saved and sanctified, but if I really wanted to serve God then I needed to get filled with the Holy Spirit, so...I did. It was like—whatever you got, I'll take it. For about six months I was a licensed Assemblies of God minister and ordained by the Conservative Baptist Association at the same time. If you know a little about their theologies, you will realize that I was not fitting in anywhere. But I just wanted God.

Despite all of these wonderful experiences, and I do not wish to put any of them down, I still felt as if it was not all fitting together. Something was not quite right. Something was missing. The blessing, the Magic, was very sporadic. Even my sense of God and His love was real only sometimes. I was hungry for the love I had felt that night at Teen Challenge. Where was it?

After I left Teen Challenge to become a pastor, I came to the church with the feeling that this would be a very short stay. There were two reasons: First, I was only supposed to be an interim pastor until they found a full-time minister. Second, I thought God had other more exciting and more important things for me to do. He would not leave me on the shelf for long. Then I met Fred and Edith Kurtz.

Fred and Edith were at the church when I went there on the Saturday morning before my first Sunday. They had been missionaries to India for many years and were now retired and in their seventies. Fred was the church custodian, and Edith was the church secretary.

I will never forget the look of childlike joy and anticipation that I met in their eyes that morning. I do not think I have ever been quite so humbled. I might have seen this as a temporary, second-rate assignment from God, but in their eyes I saw the hope that the Lord had now answered their prayers to end the turmoil and frustration the church had been through the previous year. In that humbling instant I saw that I had better change my attitude and try to serve God and the people of this church with all my heart.

In Fred and Edith I would experience the most selfless and dedicated Christians I have ever seen. They embodied the very Magic and love this book is about. So humble, so childlike, so trusting of their Lord, and yet they would have been embarrassed to death by the very words I have just written.

I entered into the ministry at Ridgeland with enthusiasm. It was a wonderful change from having been on call twenty-four hours a day at Teen Challenge. The pace was slower, they were wonderful people, and there was positive response to my messages.

The honeymoon did not last. Several members wanted to know more about the baptism of the Holy Spirit, which they knew was a vital part of the Teen Challenge ministry. Other members were adamantly opposed to that sort of thing—they did not understand it and felt that "being saved" was all that mattered. The church was becoming divided. And severe marital problems began surfacing.

Sharon has always insisted that she never really wanted to marry me, that she felt pressured into it. Now, without the intense pace and excitement of Teen Challenge, it appeared that those feelings were resurfacing. She made it clear that she wished we had never married—that she did not really love me.

In the midst of all of this, I began to burn out. Like all burn-outs, I was trying very hard to succeed. I wanted to be the minister of the whole church, not just those on one side of the issues. Every time someone would leave I was stung by it. Then, I started having anxiety attacks.

I wanted so much for that church to be united and strong in its faith. It seemed that often the people I reached out to the most were the ones who eventually left. It all began to wear me down. Perhaps I should have gone with one side or the other, but I knew I was there to be the minister of all the people.

Then came the night that I later would think of as the one that sealed our doom. The deacon board of the church had held several meetings to decide what we were going to do about the division that was growing in the church over differences in regard to the work of the Holy Spirit. Some wanted us to become a very Pentecostal-type church; others felt our tradition should continue to be Baptist in perspective. (If you are not familiar with these divisions, just realize that it involved very strong emotions on both sides.)

After more than an hour of debate, dear Fred Kurtz began to read to us from the Bible. With tears streaming down his cheeks he read Paul's words to a church of long ago, pleading with them to be united in their love and commitment to one another—telling them that this was the only thing he wanted from them.

> Make my joy complete by being of the same mind, maintaining the same love, united in spirit, intent on one purpose.
> Do nothing from selfishness or empty conceit, but with humility of mind let each of you regard one another as more important than himself. (Philippians 2: 2-3 NASB)

I felt that God was speaking directly to us through Fred. Instead of fighting for our own viewpoint, we should be doing all within our power to nurture and encourage those who saw things differently. Those who loved "red hymnals" should be pushing to get the "blue hymnals" because they knew how much it would mean to those who love the blue hymnals. And, those who love blue hymnals should be fighting just as hard to get the red for their dear brothers and sisters who loved red hymnals.

It never happened. Red fought for red, blue fought for blue, and the church never would unite in a love willing to give preference one to another.

I began to feel more and more anxiety, less and less hope, and I began to face anxiety attacks almost weekly. Something had to give. I felt as if I was sinking into a pit of miry clay.

Then came the opportunity to attend a conference in Toronto to hear a man named Len Evans. I felt that he had a message that might bring healing to our church. Instead, it brought the beginning of healing to me.

Actually, I had first heard Len speak at a Full Gospel Business Men's breakfast while I was a student at RWC. I was struck by what he said, but it seemed too simple. It was not as exciting as *The Cross and the Switchblade*. It was nice, but I wanted to be a powerful minister.

Now I wanted to explore his teachings again. I called him and found out that he would be speaking at a church in Toronto for three days. I labeled it as my conference for the year, and Sharon and I headed for Toronto.

I would not have expected it, but when we came back from those days with Len my heart was filled with joy, excitement, and peace all at the same time. I felt like jumping for joy. I knew that I had found what had been missing. And Sharon also seemed to be excited with what we had heard. Perhaps there was hope for our marriage.

This was when I first began to believe that the Christian life can be filled with incredible Magic—every day. Throughout his talks, Len would keep saying, "Ain't it fun!" And he believed it. I absolutely adored him and his message. It was not just what he taught; it was the way he lived. He took time for Sharon and me. He took us out to dinner to explain to us and model for us the message that had so transformed his life. It was a message of love given in love by this slightly round preacher whose eyes sparkled with joy. And now, the touch of God's love that night at Teen Challenge seemed within my grasp.

There was such love in those three days that Sharon and I even became romantic. We were staying at the Seaway Motel and spent time playing on the swings at the park across the street along Lake Ontario. We took walks. We bought Chinese takeout and went on a picnic together.

As a minister, you get to know other ministers. This one said that he truly believed he was the happiest man alive. Most ministers I knew at the time were struggling in many ways. I have never lost the hunger for the Magic I saw and felt in those days with Len.

It would be nice to say that from then on, all was well. It was not. This was a beginning. The teachings of those three days put me on a path and gave me some starting principles on which to build. It brought a clear and powerful focus to the teachings of Jesus and His followers. I knew I had found the key to what Jesus meant when He stated that He had come to bring us abundant, overflowing life. I had found the key to Magic.

There was much yet to learn, many more teachers to wrestle with, difficult learning experiences to go through, but the struggle would be worth it all as I discovered a path that delivers all that it promises! So can you. You really can!

What does God want from me? What will please Him? One thing!

The New Commandment

In John 13, the greatest teacher and counselor of all summarized all of His teachings into one statement, one commandment.

This is the Creator speaking; He was there from the very beginning. He knows humankind as no other being could. We are His.

So, when He makes a new statement, gives us a new word, it must be the key to life, and it is. What was it that filled my heart with joy and new hope during those three days? It was the realization that there is a way to experience life and love to the fullest that involves the simple task of endeavoring to follow one simple commandment. When Jesus, the very Creator and sustainer of life, gave us the New Commandment, He was giving us the very key to life!

A new commandment I give to you, that you love and care for one another in the same way and to the same degree that I have loved and cared for you. This is how people will know you are my disciples, if you have this love for one another. (John 13:34-35, author's paraphrase)

Much of my life has been spent in trying to please God and others by trying to do what I thought He wanted. What a freedom to see that what He wants is clear (not easy, but clear) and to see that it is a guaranteed path to joyful and fulfilling life.

This is what God wants. This is the commandment. This is what will set us apart as His. "By this all will know you are my disciples." (NASB)

And, of course, it makes so much sense that the God who is Love, who I had known as pure love, would want that very thing from us. If He had any expectations of us it would certainly be that we love, because He is Love. And now, I began to see that loving expectation everywhere I looked in the Bible.

In reading the Gospels, the parts of the Bible that describe the life of Jesus, we see a love that responded to human need wherever He encountered it. He loved the rich, the poor, the sick, and the defiant. Time and time again He used His miraculous power to heal and relieve suffering. Finally, He laid down His life for us, and even at the very end, asked His Father to forgive those who had killed Him.

Now I saw that what He wanted from me was that I try to love others in the same way He had loved me. I was to live out the powerful, consuming love I had encountered that night at Teen Challenge.

And it was in so many other places in the Bible. How had I missed it?

One of Jesus' greatest followers, the apostle Paul, taught the same thing. In one of his greatest letters, he wrote:

Owe nothing to anyone except to love one another for he who loves his neighbor has fulfilled the law. For this, "YOU SHALL NOT COMMIT ADULTERY, YOU SHALL NOT MURDER, YOU SHALL NOT STEAL, YOU SHALL NOT COVET," and if there is any other commandment it is summed up in the saying, "YOU SHALL LOVE YOUR NEIGHBOR AS YOURSELF." Love does no wrong to a neighbor, love therefore is the fulfillment of the law. (Romans 13:8-10 NASB)

Paul declares in this passage that the one who loves his neighbor as he loves himself has fulfilled the law. That means the whole law!

But how can that be? How could that do it? Because love does not do anything wrong in relationship to a neighbor, therefore it fulfills the law, even the Ten Commandments. He mentions those laws that have to do with wrong done in relationships. Love does not do these things; it therefore fulfills the law. In the Sermon on the Mount, Jesus says exactly the same thing when He talks about the narrow way and the Golden Rule.

Jesus warned us to "Enter by the narrow gate, for the gate is wide, and the way is broad that leads to destruction, and many are those who enter it." He then said "For the gate is small, and the way is narrow that leads to life, and few are those who find it." (Matthew 5:13-14 NASB)

What is the narrow way? It is very important to define because Jesus says that it is the only way that leads to life. Also, He says that not very many of us are going to find it. The other way leads to death and destruction.

I used to think that the narrow way meant walking a tightrope with God, trying to follow a bunch of rules and regulations. But God wants only one thing. Fortunately, I was challenged by Len Evans to look at Jesus' statement preceding this warning about the narrow way.

Therefore, whatever you want others to do for you, do so for them, for this is the law and the prophets. (Matthew 5:12 NASB)

This is the same message. Whatever you want others to do for you, how you would like to be treated by them, you do it first. Treat them the way you would like to be treated.

Jesus declares that what we know as the Golden Rule is the law and the prophets. To love and care for you as I would like to be loved and treated fulfills all the commands, laws, and prophets of the entire Old Testament. This is what God really wants.

Is it really this simple? Yes. It is not "religion" God wants; it is love in our relationships.

Christ said to the scribes and Pharisees: "Go and learn what this means, 'I desire mercy, not sacrifice'" (Matthew 9:13 NIV)

God is not impressed by what we try to give up for Him, nor is He impressed by our religion. He is greatly interested in how we treat one another. God desires mercy and compassion for others not sacrifice.

It even helped me to understand being "saved." Some of us have very negative reactions to Christians telling us we need to get "saved." Rightly understood, it is a valid concept. I now understood, however, what I was saved for! Peter, that wonderful disciple of Jesus, expressed what God has in mind for us when He tries to "save" us and tries to bring us to Himself.

Peter wrote, "Now that you have purified yourselves by obeying the truth so that you have sincere love for your brothers, love one another deeply, from the heart." (I Peter 1:22 NIV)

Jesus says it, Paul says it, and now Peter.

Since you have obeyed the truth and thus received love in your hearts, and since that was the purpose of being purified, see now that you use the love! And He begins to show us what is called for: fervently, with all your heart, with all your power.

The original word means to be fully extended, stretched out. I picture it like a wide receiver in football who slants across the middle to catch a pass. The ball comes at him high. He has to reach up, stretch himself, and make himself totally vulnerable to a hit from a defensive back—but that is what is required. That is what I see as Peter tells us to be fully extended in our love for each other.

I headed home from that conference with a new sense of hope and purpose. God wanted me to love those people, all of them. That was what He wanted from me, and that was what He was going to get.

I looked at it as an adventure. What was going to happen if I dropped all of the "religion" and just loved and accepted people for who they were? How would they respond to this message? Would they truly love one another so much that the divisions could begin to heal? It was almost as if I had a new guidance system.

The impact that significant others have upon our lives is related to what we feel we must do in order to gain approval. All my life I had been trying to gain everyone's approval. What an impossible task! It was like signing up for burnout. Add to that a strong desire to gain God's approval, and you get an idea of the kind of stress I was placing upon myself.

All of us live with messages from significant others who helped to shape our lives. I use the term "significant others" as it was originally coined by Dr. Harry S. Sullivan. They are the parents, family members, and significant adults who impact our lives, our self-image and our sense of what is right. They formed the dos and don'ts that we live with on a daily basis. Some of us, no matter how hard we tried, never seemed to get their approval; some of us still live to gain the approval of significant others who are long dead. We never focus on what we want and what gives value to our life. We become completely focused on external feedback and may lose ourselves in the process.

I had been given a glimpse of true freedom. Jesus said, "You will know the truth and the truth will set you free" (John 8:32 NIV). I sensed that my significance as a person would come from being who God had created me to be, and the starting point was not in trying to please all those significant others. Instead the starting point was the New Commandment and the love message of Jesus that flows from it.

I began to try to love others as Jesus loves me, with an openness and sense of caring. I stopped trying to change everything and everybody and just loved them. With a growing sense of joy, I started in fact to experience the very Magic I had sensed in Toronto. Life was becoming magical.

The times following that conference were an amazing mix of joy and discouragement, hope and despair. I was convinced that I had found the key to an exciting and life-giving church. As I came back and started sharing what I found so exciting, many began to respond in a beautiful way. The church grew in love and acceptance. Many young people began to attend as they found love and acceptance. Wounded Christians began to come and find healing.

I was thrilled with what was happening. We had a greeting time in the middle of the service when I encouraged people to say hello to others. The first week, it lasted all of fifteen seconds. Within a few months, I could not get people back into their seats after ten minutes; they were enjoying the fellowship with one another too much to stop. I felt that God was thrilled.

Most pleasing to me were the various types of people that began to come. One area of frustrations had been the women who wanted so much for their husbands to join them in the church. As this sense of unconditional love grew, some of the husbands started to attend. Their wives had begun to see in the love commandment that they were to love their husbands without the hidden agenda of changing them. In that freedom, some husbands began to come and find out that church was not such a horrible place.

A few years later, a woman named Paula ran up to me at a Young Life banquet and reintroduced herself to me. She had been a part of our church during the time I am now describing. It was wonderful to see her and hear how the Lord had blessed her life in the following years.

Paula took me over and introduced me to her husband, saying, "This is the minister who taught me to just love and accept you rather than trying to make you a Christian." And now they are joyfully serving the Lord together.

I was thrilled to see a number of people who became part of the church family who would not have been attending church were it not for a place like Ridgeland. We just loved them, and many, like Kate, began to respond and open their hearts to the Lord.

Kate was one of the loveliest and most unique individuals that had ever come to our church. She came during a period of time when many of us were taking the love message of Jesus very seriously. We were definitely growing in love, and it was becoming evident in the life of the church. As a result, many interesting people from a variety of backgrounds were being drawn to us. Kate was one of them.

Kate had met one of the young men in our church at a nightclub. He had invited her to come to church with him, so she did. She was divorced and raising two young daughters on her own. She also was doing a lot of searching, which was manifested in her dress and lifestyle.

She started coming to everything, including two small groups a week. At the same time she continued to do the kinds of things many were doing in the late '70s. She was living in two very different worlds, and now she had a problem.

She was being accepted and loved by the people of the church, and she knew that. No one was confronting her or judging her. We just loved her.

One afternoon, following a small-group Bible study, she sat with me sharing her dilemma. She had begun to realize that many aspects of her lifestyle did not fit some of the values she was encountering at the church. She realized that some of the things she was doing were not pleasing to God and were things we could not support. She did not, however, at that point feel any great desire to change.

As she shared this with me, she was clearly struggling. "I don't really want to change, but I'm afraid that you people will ask me to leave. But how can I leave these people? How can I walk away from this love?"

Notice her dilemma was not that she had realized she was living a terrible life, and we had convinced her by preaching at her that she needed to change. She caught a glimpse of a love that she did not want to walk away from. No one had told her she had to change; no one had "confronted" her. She just wanted that love and wanted to continue to be a part of us.

She never did leave. Today she is married to that young man who originally invited her to church, and they both are following the Lord. They are now very active in ministering to teens in their church.

I believe with all my heart that any fellowship that will totally commit itself to the message of love and the discoveries we were making will not be able to keep people away! They will be drawn just as Kate was to a love they have longed for all their lives even though they did not know His name.

Many very talented people were coming. Musicians and artists and even dancers were encouraged to praise the Lord with their gifts and talents. People, including me, were writing songs and teaching them to the congregation.

The variety of people was exciting. Engineers from Xerox and Kodak, a gas-station owner, an attorney, a salesman, a homemaker, a college student, a linguistics professor—all would be sitting together in one small group studying the Bible.

And the personalities—John, a former Marine who served in Vietnam and warned me that he would only come about every other week. He was soon coming to everything. Tom—who held God at arm's length for such a long time. Finally, through the encouragement of one of the church leaders who stuck with him through everything, he made a tentative commitment of his life that grew into an exciting walk with God.

We did not lay down rules. We loved people and let God change them. Some, like John and Tom, were not conforming to others' ideas of what a good church member should be, but their love for God grew. (And they were a lot more fun to be with than the "model" church member.) With Tom, I had one of the most exciting teaching experiences of my life. He had never read the Bible and asked if we could meet once a week to discuss assigned portions until he had read the entire New Testament. I therefore had the fun of seeing the Bible through the thoughts and questions of an intelligent and discerning man reading it for the first time. When, for example, the character Saul entered the book of Acts, Tom said, "I suppose this guy Saul is going to become a 'somebody'." I learned so much from the fresh insights and questions that he raised.

We started forming small groups so that we might develop our love for each other even further. Far from becoming an ingrown church, more and more people were coming as they heard about the church from friends.

As we emphasized loving each other, people began to discover the sheer joy of giving. We had always had a deacon's fund to help people with material needs, but it had been very meager. It grew tremendously. Even though we were a small church, we were able to help people in fairly substantial ways when they faced difficult financial times.

And the bottom line was that people's lives were being changed as the Lord became more and more real to them. In their own way, these days were even more exciting than the days of Teen Challenge.

And then strange things began to happen.

The more traditional people were having a hard time with the fact that most of the new people wanted a more contemporary service. Others were wondering when I was going to start getting deeper in God, get beyond this love stuff to the great truths of God. Still others wanted more of an emphasis on the gifts and power of the Holy Spirit. And my heart began to break as the walls separating us seemed to get higher and higher. Even some of those who were attracted to the church because of the love and fellowship now wanted to get on to something more mature and spiritual. They wanted balance. Some even said that we were just having too much fun.

But for me there wasn't anything deeper. Paul says to Timothy that the goal of your teaching and instructing is love. As far as I could see, we were finally on our way toward the goal (see 1Timothy 1:5).

The pressure grew. Did I have the right message? I felt I did. The apostle John, perhaps Jesus' closest disciple, declares that this has been our message since the beginning.

> For this is the message which you have heard from the beginning, that we should love one another...we know that we have passed out of death into life, because we love the brethren. He who does not love, abides in death. (1 John 3:11,14 NASB)

When the apostle John wrote this letter, it may have been as many as fifty years since the time he first heard the New Commandment. He was still talking about it. In fact, if you read this letter, you will find that John was still filled with excitement over the joy of life with Jesus and with other Christians who had discovered this love. He still had Magic!

So now, so many years later, John again asks these Christians to focus on this word they have had from the very beginning. Such is this message's great importance.

I said that this New Commandment is the key to life. I was not kidding. "We know that we have passed out of death into life, because we love our fellow Christians."

Have you passed out of death into life? Are you really alive? John says I can determine the answers by how we love! For a long time I did not see this incredible truth. How do I know I am a part of God's kingdom? Have I passed from death to life because I have had a certain religious experience? Have I passed from death to life if I belong to a certain church or because I go to church? Have I passed from death to life because I have made great sacrifices for God?

John says it is because I love you! In fact, if I do not love, I remain in death! It is very simple. If I really want to live I can start by loving you.

So, I continued to point people to this truth: You can begin now, wherever you are, whatever your circumstances, to walk in this love. Your life and the lives of those around you will never be the same.

Where do you begin? With those who are closest to you. My own study of the Bible leads me to believe that these are the priorities:

Your spouse, your children, others in your family, your brothers and sister in the Lord. Finally, all people.

So where do you get this love? If you are a part of God's family, if you have opened your life up to Him, then you already have it. You may not always feel it, but it is there.

The same love the Father has for the Son is in you. Jesus prayed for exactly that the night before He died.

Your part, then, is to begin to act upon that love, to begin to show that love to others.

Many of us, because of a negative sense of self, are caught when we try to experience God as a God of love who sees us as highly valued persons. That truth cannot seem to break through all the negative messages of a lifetime.

What can we do? We can begin to act on truth, regardless of previous negative reinforcement. Showing love and concern for others as Jesus commands may be the very beginning of realizing your true value and worth.

It means we stop focusing on what people have told us about ourselves, and we look at what Jesus says. We do it. We go out of our way for someone else, we give a warm greeting, a cup of cold water, ten minutes of true listening—and something just may start to happen. That flow of love just might begin. You just might find a narrow path that leads to life.

As I continued my discovery, I was struck by much more than the fact that this love commandment was all over the New Testament. I also saw an intensity toward it that exceeded that of any other topics.

For example, I saw it in one of Paul's letters.

The church of Thessalonica was a mature church. Paul was very pleased with the church's spiritual growth. We find in his first letter to them none of the great concern he expressed in other letters to the churches of Corinth and Galatia. Instead Paul expresses great thanksgiving as he thinks of them.

Notice the powerful call Paul places upon this already maturing church.

And may the Lord cause you to increase and abound in love for one another and for all... (1 Thessalonians. 3:12 NASB)

Paul has already thanked God for their labors of love. But Paul wants them to do more! He wants them to abound and overflow in their love for each other!

Paul reaches a great intensity. In fact at one point, he states that they do not even need to be taught about loving one another. They are already practicing it. They practice it toward all of their fellow Christians in that area. Surely they have arrived.

But no; Paul exhorts them to excel still more! And the phrasing of the original language means more and more and more and more, as long as you want to say it (see 1 Thessalonians. 4:9-10).

It was almost frightening to see what these New Testament writers were proclaiming. John says it's our call from the beginning. Peter says to love each other fervently, and Paul tells us to abound, overflow, and excel—and then to do it still more!

This is a very different "tape" from the ones most of us grew up with, whether we were reared in a Christian home or not.

What is right? What is success? What pleases God? What does it mean to really live? What does it mean to be Christian in character? What should be the priorities of my life? What should be my goals for personal growth?

All of these questions and more are inexorably altered when I see them in light of the New Commandment.

I was coming alive. Magic was pouring in. No longer was I focusing on dos and don'ts. No longer was I focusing on what others considered Christian or successful. I could now begin to feel the pleasure and yes, approval, of God when I took the time to sit in a nursing home talking to one of His elderly children as much—no, more—than when I gave a good sermon for hundreds of people during a church service.

How would your life be changed if you took this commandment seriously? What would happen if you started to love others with all of your might? What if a church started to do that? That's what I was trying to find out.

I continued to teach what I was finding in the Bible, and the opposition continued to mount. What a contrast! One group growing in love and joy—the other group getting more and more frustrated with this love stuff.

"We are not moving on to maturity" was a main complaint. "We have to keep aware of God's holiness."

So, I preached on the holiest man alive! We took a look at the most upright man on earth. How would you feel if someone said that you are the most upright person on earth? How would you feel if God Himself said that you are the most upright person on earth? This is what God said about Job.

Why did God say this? What was it about Job that pleased Him so much? What would the life of a man who so pleased God be like? What does it mean to be this upright?

In chapter 29 of the Old Testament book of Job, Job looks back over his life and reflects on the time when his life was richly blessed. At present, he is going through a terrible time of distress, but his reflection gives us a portrait of the life of the most righteous person alive.

First, Job speaks about a very special relationship with the God who is Love. He talks of having the friendship of God over the tent of his life. This describes a relationship of true warmth and intimacy. A personal relationship with God is the key to a life of true righteousness.

But then he describes for us how that relationship worked in his everyday living. Here we begin to see what has so impressed God about this man Job.

Job's life was a life of caring deeply about the needs of his fellow human being. This is what God loves; this is what He always wants from us.

Look at Job's life: "I was eyes to the blind, feet to the lame.... I made the widow's heart to sing" (Job 29: 15, 13 NASB).

Job is seen as a man who took action. He loved with his deeds, not just with his words. Those in his community were directly helped by him. The orphans, the widowed, the handicapped, and many others knew Job as one who helped to ease their burdens.

The text continues: "Because I delivered the poor who cried for help And the orphan who had no helper I was a father to the needy" (Job 29: 12, 16 NASB).

His care went beyond those needs that were apparent to him. Perhaps we find ourselves overwhelmed by needs we already know about, but Job tried to find even more needy folks! "I investigated the case which I did not know" (Job 29:16 NASB).

Not only did Job love others, but he also was continually trying to find more opportunities to love. No wonder God was so pleased, and no wonder he had such a friendship with God.

This is a portrait of true holiness and righteousness. In his letter to the Thessalonians, Paul writes, "May the Lord cause you to increase and abound in love for one another…so that He may establish your hearts unblamable in holiness…" (1 Thessalonians 3:12-13 NASB).

True holiness is not a monastic existence; it is not about avoiding smoking, dancing, and chewing, as the saying goes. It is not a legalistic following. True holiness is a life increasing in and overflowing with love for all people.

Job did just that—and God said he was the most upright person on the face of the earth.

When I saw this, it became even more evident what it is that God really wants from me.

It is also very important to see that this love was not a weak love. True love is concerned not only with showing mercy and kindness, but it is also very concerned with justice.

Job would take powerful action against those who were mistreating their fellow human beings: "I broke the jaws of the wicked and snatched the prey from his teeth" (Job 29:17 NASB).

It is not always enough to be nice. Sometimes we too may take powerful action against those who would steal from and devour others.

What did this mean in my own walk of faith? My priorities were changing! I again saw what God was showing me. God was more impressed with how I responded to people's needs than He was with all my religious activity. And that was the basis for true friendship with this beloved Lord: The one who loves knows God (in an intimate and personal way).

I saw what God thought of Job's life; what might He think of mine? Again, it was very different from many of my old tapes regarding approval. As I began to try in some new ways to practice it, I saw that I did indeed begin to sense a new closeness and joy in my relationship with God. My walk of faith was coming alive in a whole new way.

Those who were responding to the message of love were finding greater and greater joy. Jesus said, "You shall know the truth, and the truth shall make you free" (John 8:32 NASB).

Time and again I was being challenged by members who wanted me to stop talking so much about loving one another and to start talking more about loving God. They insisted that we must love God first.

In Toronto, Len Evans had challenged me to try a simple exercise. He encouraged me to notice as I read the New Testament that while it mentions once in a while that we are to love God, on almost every page we are given something relative to loving one another. Why? Why this emphasis? If my teaching was out of balance, at least I was in good company.

But you see, it was not out of balance—love is the balance. There is ultimately only one way to express my love for God.

Someone has said that the genius of Jesus was that He took the two greatest commandments, combined them into one, and lost nothing of the first two. I believe that. At one point, Jesus was asked to name the greatest commandment. He responded:

> "You shall love the Lord your God with all your heart, and with all your soul, and with all your mind." This is the great and foremost commandment. The second is like it, "You shall love your neighbor as yourself." (Matthew 22:37-39 NASB)

Here, Jesus tells us what the two greatest commandments are. But He was asked to give one. Why does He give two? Because the second gives definition and content to the first.

The primary way that I show love for God is by loving you. How else could I love God? What does He need from me? Nothing.

What does He want from me? What we have been looking at: mercy, justice, and love toward my fellow human being.

This is the completion of the flow of this great Magic and love.

Once Jesus was talking about that day when we will all stand in the presence of God—what some call the Day of Judgment. He described the scene as a shepherd separating his flock, the sheep from the goats. To those He invites to be a part of His kingdom forever, He says: "I was hungry, and you gave Me food to eat; I was thirsty, and you gave Me a drink; I was a lonely stranger, and you invited Me into your home; I had no clothing, and you clothed Me; when I was sick, you visited Me, and when I was in prison, you came to see Me" (Matthew 25:35-36, author's paraphrase).

They are astonished. They say, "When did we do that for You, our Lord and King?" And Jesus said the response will be: "As you were doing this for My brothers and sisters, even those who were extremely insignificant, you were doing it to and for Me" (see Matthew 25:37-40).

Astounding! This completes the cycle. When I show love to you, I am in fact loving God.

Imagine! Every hour of every day you and I have opportunities to show love to God. Our lives are filled with magical opportunities. He comes to us in the form of our spouse, our children, our coworkers, our friends, our enemies. Every time we show love to them, we are loving God. It is sobering to realize that when we fail to do that, we have failed to love Him.

He also said that day: "In as much as you did show love, or did not show love to the most insignificant person you know, that is how you did or did not show love to Me" (see Matthew 25:45).

People all over the world, all around us, are endeavoring to love God, to be religious. Jesus is telling us that the way to truly do that is to show love to those in need. Nothing less, no matter how religious or sacrificial, will do.

What are the implications of this passage? To me there are two:

First, it is frightening; what an awesome responsibility! How much easier to obey a few rules and go to church. How do I face the fact that to ignore someone in need is the same as ignoring Jesus – the One who has such love for me?

Second, it holds the potential of making all of life joyful, sacred, and meaningful! Not one day will have to be boring or insignificant. Every day there will be a chance to give love to Jesus. No wonder Jesus could proclaim that even a cup of cold water given in His name would have eternal significance.

How did this impact me? For one thing, I saw that I could put my arms around God every day in the most enjoyable and fun-filled ways you can imagine. And, while having this fun, I could also be touching upon greatness in the kingdom of God.

One day the disciples were arguing about which one of them was the greatest. When they arrived at their destination Jesus began to ask them about it. There was an embarrassed silence. Jesus told them that if they wanted to be first, they must be as a slave/servant to all others. Then, to illustrate, He took a child up into His arms and said:

"Whoever receives one child like this in My name is receiving Me; and whoever receives me is not receiving me, but Him who sent me." (Mark 9:37 NASB)

Hear what Jesus is saying. The disciples wanted to know which one of them would be the greatest. They were so human! And this was not the only time they had this discussion.

So, Jesus takes a little child and sets him in the middle of the group. In that culture, a child was not terribly significant. So there he stands.

Then Jesus makes a statement that many of us read right past. He tells us how to love God. In essence, He says, "Anyone who receives this child into his arms just hugs him; when you do that, you have put your arms of loving acceptance around Me. And not just me but the Father who sent me." Do you want to hug God today? Find a small child, perhaps your own, and hug and love that child. You will be holding the Son and the Father in your arms. Magic!

Do you see now why I believe that the New Commandment fulfills all commandments, including the one to love God?

This truth hit me late one afternoon. I was heading out to a church meeting, when my then two-year-old son, Jason, looked at me and said, "You got your bye-bye book, Daddy?"

I looked down, and there in my hand was my Bible. I almost always took it with me to the variety of meetings that kept me away from home several nights each week. I was appalled that my son equated this book, which is so special, with a sign that his dad was leaving again.

So often, those of us in the ministry and in the work of the church have been guilty of rushing by our children (i.e., Jesus) on our way out the door to serve God. I knew I had to make some changes in my priorities.

This was a joyful lesson. I love my three children so much, and now I saw that to love God would mean to love them! It was like getting paid spiritually for something I wanted to do anyway. This was one of many implications I would see coming out the Magic key that makes people our first priority.

I was convinced with all my heart that I had found the key to the universe, the key to knowing daily the presence of the One who is Love. His loving expectation of me was that as I received His wonderful love, I would then share that love with others, and in doing that I would be loving Him. I believed it. I still believe it, but I was about to hit an incredible and horrible detour.

CHAPTER FIVE

Unconditional Love

I Lose It, Big Time

Now comes the hard part. In a way, I wish I could tell my story without this section. I wish I could talk about never-ending success, but that is not what happened. And I have often complained about the unreality of Christian books that make it look as if life is one victory after another. So I hope you will stay with me as I talk about my most difficult days and my biggest failures.

The church I pastored was dividing almost in half. About half were thrilled over what was happening, and about half were getting stronger in their demand for something deeper or something more traditional or something more charismatic or something more evangelistic. The pressure and the heartbreak became enormous.

On top of all of that, my marriage problems had resurfaced and were escalating. Sharon had decided that since she was not in a marriage that could bring her fulfillment she needed other things. She started and ran a successful daycare center. She became a successful real estate agent. She tried several small business ventures. As time went on she was busier and busier with these other ventures. And I got angrier and angrier over these circumstances.

I discovered that there were others who would give me the time, attention, and reinforcement that I was not getting from her. Discouraged about the church, frustrated and angry over my marriage relationship, my focus drifted away from the Lord to other things, some that were OK, and some that definitely were not. I became more and more involved in coaching Karen's Little League baseball teams. Three summers I coached two teams instead of just one. In a way, that was my emotional salvation; in another way it kept me from facing and dealing with important issues.

I had never lost that desire for the love promised by the god of Eros in my teenage years. It became very obvious I would not have that with Sharon. She truly believed she had not loved me in that way and never would. A few others assured me in subtle and not so subtle ways that I was someone they could love in that way. It felt wonderful to know that. Getting attention from attractive young ladies had always been wonderful for my self-esteem, but it threw the priorities of my life into a hellish confusion. The god of Eros was fighting for first place, promising me the self-esteem I never had as a teenager, promising shortcuts to happiness, trying to destroy me and others.

This went on for a couple of years. I would explode at Sharon for living her life elsewhere. She would feel even more justified in needing to have something else to live for, and I was disobeying God by looking to others for the esteem I wanted from her. What a mess. I failed the Lord terribly.

I am not sure exactly why or how, but I pulled out of that cycle, repented, and started to rededicate myself to the Lord. I renewed my commitment to Sharon (although she did not really want it) and tried to be more understanding of what it would mean to love her on her terms, not mine. Unfortunately,

I became even more possessive, more demanding, and more upset that she felt I would never be the one for her.

Things began to move forward at the church again. My marriage was not fulfilling, but at least I knew I was trying my best again to please God. I had shared with the church family that I had failed the Lord and them, asked their forgiveness, and was moving ahead.

But it just did not work. Some who knew the problems Sharon and I were having felt that I could not pastor if I could not have a marriage that was a good example. Some still wanted me to get off all that love stuff. Some wanted us to become much more charismatic in our worship. One of the most difficult problems was the fact that one of the church leaders I was close to decided that I just was not spiritual enough to be leading the church. He strongly questioned my relationship to God. The irony was that he was right, but he was two years late—I had renewed my relationship to God two years before. No matter what I did, he continued to question my walk with God. And actually, I don't blame him. I had disappointed him terribly.

Almost weekly, Sharon was telling me that she was going to leave. Some people felt that it was time to take a vote to force me from the church. It was the worst time in my life.

Here I was, a man who at age sixteen knew that he was to be a minister, at the age of twenty-two had started a very successful Teen Challenge Center, had pastored for fourteen years—now, my hope was gone. I could see no way out, no answers. Even my belief in myself was fading. I never felt so alone.

One of the major issues I had to deal with as my world began to unravel was my foundational belief that God is Love. I knew very well that my own sin had brought on many of my difficulties, but there was much more to it than that. I found myself questioning who God is. What is He really like?

This was not a small issue. If He was the way many people in the church were telling me He was, then I was not sure I wanted to have much to do with Him. I held Him at arm's length for a long time. On an emotional level I had begun to fear that God was not very understanding or compassionate, perhaps not even very forgiving. It was a period of great despair. What I had taken for granted had eroded to the point that I was now quite content to avoid any direct contact with God or His people.

As it became clear that my marriage was deteriorating and as pressure was mounting to resign from the church, I sought help through counseling from a dear Christian man named Phil Geibel. Through painful sessions, I shared with him what I was experiencing.

One day we were talking about letting go, that perhaps it was time to realize that if my wife truly wished to leave, then maybe that was what must happen. We were also talking about the next step in my life. What did God have planned for me?

Working with Phil is sort of like working with Lieutenant Columbo of the 1970s TV series—he just gets these hunches. He pointed out to me that as we were talking about praying, a strange smile had crossed my face—almost as if I had been caught doing something wrong. What was that all about? I was not sure. But as we explored that further it began to dawn on me that I had very little intention of asking God about anything. Why? Because I had begun at a certain level to buy into a new concept of God. I realized that for me at this stage of my life turning to God did not mean turning to the loving Father I had known all my life but turning to a God who was like Tash in *The Chronicles of Narnia*.

In that series of books by C.S. Lewis, the great lion Aslan represents the love and wisdom of Jesus. But there is another "god" named Tash. He is sort of like a huge vulture who lays heavy burdens and rules upon his followers as he uses them totally for his own ends. As Phil and I continued to talk, suddenly the thought leaped into my mind: God is not Tash! I was shocked to realize how much I had begun to doubt the love and goodness of God.

I had allowed some very difficult circumstances to slowly move me toward seeing God as Tash. Try as I would, my marriage was not going to make it. I had sincerely asked the church to forgive me for the sin and disobedience in my own life, but no matter how hard I tried I could not get a new start with some of the leaders. Charles Swindoll has said that we Christians are the only ones who shoot our wounded; I was experiencing that. I was told, "We can forgive, but we can't forget." I guess I had started to believe that God has the same attitude. Contrary to what I had always believed it seemed that God was punishing me for my sins, sins I had repented of long ago, but like Tash He had waited for the right time to really punish me the most.

I left Phil's office that afternoon excited and scared. I now understood why I had distanced myself from God. Now I had to examine the most crucial issue I would face: Who is God, really? Tash? Aslan? Loving? Stern? Harsh? Understanding? A cruel taskmaster? A loving Father? Who is He? What did I really believe? I knew that I had to settle this question above anything else. And I had to settle it for myself. The faith that I had sort of taken for granted had been shaken to its foundation. Now I had some deep soul-searching to do.

I started by looking very closely at Jesus, especially His words in the Sermon on the Mount. It seems to me that what we have are two parallel images of God: first, in the form of Jesus, a humble, compassionate, kind, caring and forgiving teacher/carpenter from the insignificant village of Nazareth, the most humane person ever. "He who has seen Me has seen the Father" (John 14:9). Could that be true? Could the power behind atomic energy, the Creator of a seemingly infinite universe, be Him? Second is the image of a loving, caring, compassionate heavenly Father who cares deeply about each and every one of His children. He knows all about them—knows their needs, is always there for them, always listening, always ready to forgive, to answer, to guide them into the best possible life. He always holds His children in the highest possible regard.

I thought back to an evening when this had become very real to me. I was sitting at home with my family watching the movie *Ben-Hur*. I saw a reality of who God is with new eyes, the eyes of my then five-year-old son Jason.

Judah Ben-Hur was being dragged across the Israeli desert, tied to a chain gang for a crime he did not commit. The master of the chain gang had taken a particular dislike to him.

They came to a village called Nazareth, and the prisoners finally began to receive cups of water from the villagers. Ben-Hur falls to his knees waiting for water. As the cup is placed in his hands, the master of the chain gang knocks it from him, declaring that no water will be given to this prisoner.

Judah Ben-Hur falls to the ground and in total despair asks God to please help him. Suddenly we see the back of a young carpenter who stoops down and begins to give water to Ben-Hur. He halts the advance of the chain gang master with one glance and then continues to lovingly give water to Ben-Hur.

It was at this point that Jason says almost in a whisper, "Jesus is so nice." At that moment, I realized in a new way, with my heart as well as my mind, that Jason was absolutely right. Jesus is so nice...so kind...so caring...so gentle, so very, very loving.

Colossians 1:15, speaking of the Christ, says that He is "the exact likeness of the unseen God." Hebrews 1:3 says that He is "the perfect imprint and very image of God's nature" (author's paraphrase).

What I see as I read the Gospels is that Jesus loved people. He consistently reached out in love. No need was too small or too large.

"He that has seen Me has seen the Father." I looked closely at the second image—Jesus' description of the Father. Much of what He had to say is found in what we call the Sermon on the Mount. What we are looking at is perhaps the most revolutionary aspect of all the things Jesus taught.

To debate with the Pharisees about rules and traditions is one thing, but to present the character of God Himself in a way that challenges the very foundation of their religious and political institutions is quite another. And I believe that for our world today, God as presented here by the Son of God is still one of the most radical and revolutionary ideas you will ever encounter.

Why did He sacrifice His Son for you? How could He let His Son be killed for me?

Because He is Love!

What do we learn about God from Jesus' teaching?

First, we learn that He is a very personal God. He is not a vague "force." He is not a computer in the sky; He is not an absentee landlord.

The Bible declares God to be a very personal being. (In fact, He is the source of our being personal creatures.) Jesus states that He is so personal and so intimately involved with our lives that He knows what we need before we can even ask Him! God is not saying that we should not bother to ask because He already knows our needs. God wants us to see that He is very aware of who we are. We never have a problem or a need that God is not concerned about. Psalm 139 states, "Thou are intimately acquainted with all my ways" (Psalm 139:3 NASB).

Some psychologists tell us that one of man's innate and powerful yearnings is the desire for an omnipotent, omniscient, and all-caring parent. Atheistic psychologists tell us that this, together with man's infinite capacity for self-deception, creates a yearning for and a belief in the super-being. This is the reason strong leaders are able to develop followings of such great magnitude.

The Christian view, however, is that this yearning is not a deception and is in fact the most natural thing in the world. It is exactly what we would expect when we see that we have been created for fellowship with a God who is such a loving and caring parent. Jesus declares that this is not deception, that this powerful yearning can be fulfilled.

We can, in fact we must, come like children to our loving Father and find the peace and joy that only a personal relationship with Him can bring. My basic faith was being renewed and confirmed as I continued to study.

God, in reality, is Love. When we reach out to Him we touch reality. If the heavens opened up to us, what would we find? What is behind all of this that our senses perceive? Behind the seemingly infinite space, behind that apparent complexity of history and philosophy, behind the confusion of the seemingly infinite and unsolvable problems of planet earth, what is the final reality, this loving Father?

That night at Teen Challenge when I had felt immersed in God's love it was a very mystical experience; God was so present. But in another way, far from being just mystical, I may have been more in touch with Reality than at any other time in my life.

In the Sermon on the Mount, Jesus teaches us about just how much the heavenly Father cares about His children.

Not only does He love us, He also cares about all the aspects of our daily lives. Jesus wants us to realize that we do not have to struggle in anxiety and worry, for we do have a Father who is omnipotent, omniscient, and all-caring. God knows us and knows that we need these things. Jesus points out that God takes care of the grass and the flowers, so of course He will take care of us. Why worry? It may seem simple to say that God is Love, but what about the implications for our daily lives?

If I believe that God is Love, that Jesus presents an honest picture here, then knowing of God's love should impact my daily thinking and living.

Very few who think of themselves as Christians would deny this truth. I never would have. But what if someone who had no bias about it simply observed our lives with some degree of access to our inner thoughts? What would that person conclude?

I believe they would observe that we talk about God as being love and say He is a loving heavenly Father who watches over us, and then take actions and think thoughts that would totally confuse the observer.

I have struggled a great deal with this (and still do). Even as God has been trying to teach me that He really is Love, I still worried as if He could not be trusted. I sometimes worry about finances, health, red lights, and other major and minor problems as much as the person who has no knowledge of God's love.

This was a real concern to Jesus. In the Sermon on the Mount, Jesus creates a beautiful picture of God. Will we believe Him? What a change it could make! I needed that now more than ever.

The third thing we learn from the Sermon on the Mount is that the Father's love is unconditional. This was crucial to my struggle!

Jesus reminds His listeners that they have been told they should love their neighbors and hate their enemies. This seems universal. We know our friends and we know our enemies, and we treat them accordingly.

But Jesus said something radical. He calls upon people to love their enemies, to even pray from them, because then they will be like children of their Father. Why? Because His love is unconditional.

He sends the blessings of His sunshine and His rain on the good and the evil. If you love only those who love you, big deal; even "sinners" do that. Be like your Father; He is Love and continues to pour out His perfect love even on those who act like His enemies.

Think of it. Here is a love that never ends. He loves me as much when I am bad as when I am good. He pours out life-giving rain and sunshine on the just and the unjust, the righteous and the wicked.

God doesn't just love those who are good and then once in a while throw a little love at the wicked to see if they are ready to straighten up. He is Love; He cannot deny Himself.

Such a concept may be hard for us to grasp. We are prone to give love based upon the response we get back. God does not.

As David Wilkerson said to gang leader Nicky Cruz on the streets of New York City, "You can cut me into a thousand pieces and every piece will say, 'Nicky, Jesus loves you.'"

We will never confront a love more potent and relentless than the love of the Father that Jesus described. Joy came back into my life. Yes, I had failed. Yes, I was facing a terrible time. But He had never stopped loving me for a moment. Not only had He forgiven, but indeed He also had forgotten. He loves unconditionally!

For one year, I served as the assistant pastor of Parkminster Presbyterian Church in Chili, New York. Most Sundays I had the responsibility of presenting the children's message. One Sunday morning I had my daughter Kathy, who is a gifted artist, write out John 3:16 on two posters with blank spaces where "the world" would be written so that it looked like the following:

For God so loved _____ that He gave His only Son so that if _____ will believe in Him, _____ will not perish, but have everlasting life.

As the children gathered around me, I pointed out to them that God knew and loved each of them and that they could write their own names in the blank spaces. Two children volunteered to do so. Just as we finished reading the poster with the name of the second volunteer written in, a question was raised. Little three-year-old Tim looked up at me with wide eyes and asked, "What about me?" His voice rang out as clear as a bell throughout the sanctuary and acted as a reminder that each of us long to be included.

Sometimes I felt like little Tim, like a child wanting to know for sure that God really does love me. He does! Then came a point in my life when that lesson from Jason started to take hold.

The phone rang at 2:45 a.m. On the other end of the line was one of the most tormented individuals I have ever encountered in all my years of counseling and pastoring. She said, "I want to kill myself!"

Over the next several months, I spent many hours talking with this troubled woman named Toni. She had left her husband as soon as her daughter had turned eighteen. Toni had been planning on this departure for almost all of her daughter's life. Now she had finally made that break but was living with such strong feelings of guilt over what she had done that she had fallen into a severe depression. I am sharing her story not because it will be a great success story but because through my groping attempts to help her, I experienced the incredible impact of what I was now rediscovering.

I somehow decided, quite incorrectly, that Toni's basic problem was that she was angry with God. She needed to see this and admit to it. So we entered a power struggle. I was convinced that she needed to humble herself and admit that her anger against God was unjustified and that she needed to ask God's forgiveness. Toni did not want to talk to God for fear He might tell her to return to her husband. Fortunately, I listened and demonstrated a caring attitude that may have helped her, in spite of my attempts to convert her. Often she was angry with me, but I was the only one she could reach in the middle of those long, depressing nights.

During this same period of time, I was beginning to understand who God really is. I was starting to believe that God is a heavenly Father who dearly loves each of His children. A phone conversation with Toni helped me to see how much I was changing because of this new understanding.

It had been almost a year since I had heard from Toni. I had even moved and changed phone numbers. I do not remember now just how we had lost contact. It had taken place gradually. Then, one evening she called. In the same depressed state, she began to talk about her situation and how totally trapped she felt. She was still being torn apart by guilt.

I did not in any conscious way decide to try a new tactic with Toni. I was not aware of the difference until the conversation was almost over. I did not talk to Toni about how angry she still was with God. I simply told her that God, who is Love, loved her very much.

She began in her own tortured way to protest that God could not possibly love her because of what she had done to her husband. I continued to assure her of His faithfulness and love. Finally, knowing how much she loved her daughter, I asked her if Margaret could ever do anything that would cause her to stop loving her. She was shocked at the question. "Of course not; how could anything stop me from loving her? She is my whole world!" "Then, Toni," I said, "don't you see that God is a parent who loves you in that same way and even more?" She was astounded. The tension and torture left her voice. Toni asked me if some tragedy had happened in my life lately. "No. Why?" I replied. "Because you are so different; what happened to you? You're so gentle and understanding!"

We talked a few more minutes. It was in these few short moments that we shared a closeness and a communication greater than all the hours before. After we said goodbye, I sat there, not quite able to put together what had just taken place. What had happened to me? I surmised that I learned that God is Love. I suppose I learned that if I could help people to see how much God cares for them, then He, not I, can do the healing and the converting.

What would happen if we all believed that? Well, I realized that one precious lady had now become aware of God's love for her and I was now different in a way that had astonished her. I was letting myself believe that "Jesus is so nice!" Now, it was time to believe it anew.

Unconditional Positive Regard

My new search was convincing me that God loves me with Unconditional Positive Regard.

What is that? Where can I find it? Does it really exist?

Most of us who have delved into the field of counseling have run into this concept of unconditional positive regard. Some feel that it is a crucial characteristic to possess in order to be an effective counselor. Others do not see it as necessary, and still others see it as total illusion.

To have unconditional positive regard means that I value you as a person of true worth, whether I agree with you and approve of your actions or not. Whatever you say or do, I will continue to respect you and hold you in high regard. In counseling, this atmosphere makes it possible for a person to be open with their true inner thoughts and struggles.

What I found a little troubling during this period was that I had in fact encountered a man who was showing me this kind of regard in a way I had never seen it. In many ways, his was the most Christlike caring for others I had seen. It was a stark contrast to what I was getting from the church.

There was only one hitch. This man, Dr. Muhyi Shakoor, was a Muslim.

Muhyi was a professor in the master's program I will talk more of later. He taught a course I was taking on group counseling. He truly demonstrated unconditional positive regard. I learned much from him.

One afternoon at the close of the semester I was sitting in his office discussing my final project. At the end of the discussion, Muhyi, who knew I was a minister, looked at me and said, "By the way, I just want you to know that I have the greatest respect for Jesus Christ." He meant it.

It was quite unsettling to see a Muslim treating people with the most Christlike respect I had ever witnessed. But that treatment was not soft. I often left this class smarting from some of the painful and loving things he had said to me, but far from turning me away from Jesus, it made me even hungrier to know and to live that kind of love. It was another aspect of rebuilding my belief that God is Love—not Tash.

I believe that God has unconditional positive regard for each and every one of us. Agape love, the Greek word used for how God loves us, means to love and value persons just because they are, not because we personally get anything (including right behavior) back from them. You are loved because you are who you are. God loves us in that way.

Think of it! You do not have to earn His love. You already have it! You do not have to get Him to like you. He already does! No matter what you say, do, or think, He will still love and cherish you. You will never lose value in His eyes.

Zephaniah 3:16-17 contains a wonderful statement regarding how God feels about us. It says: "He will rejoice over thee with gladness, He will calm all your fears with love, He will exult over thee with singing" (author's paraphrase).

Think of it. You put a happy song in the heart of God. That is how precious and special you are to Him!

Jesus gave us a beautiful illustration of the quality of the Father's love in the story we know as the Parable of the Prodigal Son.

A rich man had two sons, and at one point the younger son came to his father and asked him for his inheritance. The father gave in to the son's wishes and presented him with the money.

The son journeyed to a far country and began to use his newly acquired wealth in order to have a great time with food, drink, and women. It was not long before his money was gone and he had nothing left to live on.

Eventually the son's spirits sank so low that he hired himself out as a servant whose task was to feed the pigs on someone's farm. Here he was, the son of a very rich father, feeding food to pigs that were eating better than he was.

He began to realize what he was doing. He thought about the fact that servants in his father's house were living better than he was. He made up his mind: He would go back home, beg his father's forgiveness, and ask if he could please be allowed to labor as one of the servants.

How his heart must have trembled as he came into view of his father's house. What would happen? How would he be received?

His father saw him and recognized him when he was still far from the house. He ran to him at full speed, threw his arms around him, and wept for joy.

The father lifted him to his feet, ignored his plea to become a servant, and began giving orders to his servants to prepare a feast in celebration of the fact that his son had in essence returned from the dead!

The elder son had been away while this was taking place and upon his return began to inquire about the celebration. When the servants told him that his brother had returned and that the father had ordered a great celebration, the elder son was angry and jealous and refused to go in to the feast.

When the father heard of this, he went out to speak to his son. The elder son expressed great anger. "I have served you faithfully, and you have never given me such a party. But for this son of yours who wasted your money on harlots and evil living you prepare the fatted calf!" he said.

The father implored the son, saying, "All that you want from me is yours; you should know that, but your brother who was dead is now back with us. How could we not celebrate his return?"

What do we learn about our heavenly Father from what we see in the father of this story? Well, what leaps out at me is his forgiveness. He forgave completely. He never once berated the son about the lost inheritance. In fact, he never mentions it. He did not hold his son at arm's length saying: "Well, I sure hope you've learned your lesson this time." He just ran to him, threw his arms around him, and showered him with love! No holding back, no thoughts of never letting his son hurt him or use him again—just unconditional love, forgiveness, and...

Restoration! No probation. He threw a party and treated his son with the utmost honor and respect. All he wanted to do was to rejoice in the fact that his son had come home. All was forgiven and forgotten.

We also see other subtle qualities in the prodigal's father that are God-like. For example, when his son first approached the father about taking his inheritance, the father gave it to him freely. The prodigal's father showed unconditional love. He loved with an open hand. No thoughts of using that money to keep the love and loyalty of his son. How difficult that must have been for this father to do. There were no strings attached. He wanted the son to choose to love him, not to love him because of the inheritance.

Of course, that freedom works two ways. As the son began to destroy his life, the father who loved him so much had to wait. God will never force us to obey or do the wise thing, even when it would be for our own good. He has really given us the freedom to choose. He will, and certainly does, warn us about the consequences of the wrong choices, but the choice is ours. We can waste our inheritance and destroy our lives if we really want to.

But the Lord always waits for us. The father saw the son coming a long way off. Like the prodigal's father, God is still there, still watching for the slightest sign that we want His help.

What a blessing to know that God holds us in such high regard! He loves us with an everlasting love. He will not manipulate us. He just loves us.

We see this in the life of Jesus. He loved people. He spent much of His time with the publicans—the sinners—the outcasts. He loved and valued them.

And that is how He loves you.

Let me share with you the story of a time when I received unconditional positive regard.

It had been one of those days. I had hit bottom. I was filled with frustration, anger, and anxiety. As we are prone to do, I was taking it out on someone else. That someone else was Karen.

Early that morning, I had been through a horrendous board meeting at the church. I felt as if I was being torn apart by issues that had supposedly been settled a month before. I left the meeting feeling that it would not matter if I never saw the church again. Maybe ministers are not supposed to hurt like that, but they do. And I did.

I drove from there to coach my daughter's Little League baseball game. I don't even remember if we won or lost. I asked her to carry the baseball equipment to the car while I attended to something else. She placed it behind our station wagon. A few minutes later, we drove off without it.

On any other day, this situation would have seemed trivial, but on this day, with my emotions already drained,

I exploded when I found out what happened. I let loose on Karen for not having put the equipment into the car. As I ranted and raved, tears started spilling out of her eyes.

I drove to the field, and the equipment was gone. Great! Not only was I a failure at church, I had now proven that I had been irresponsible with five-hundred dollars' worth of baseball equipment. Perhaps you can relate to how I felt. It wasn't a great tragedy, but I felt like a total failure, and I felt totally alone.

As I headed back home, I began dreading having to call Jim Brokaw, one of the league officials, to let him know what a jerk I had been.

I got him on the phone, explained what had happened, offered to buy new equipment (though I do not know how I would have paid for it), and awaited his response.

What I received from him was incredible understanding and support. He assured me that there was no way he would expect me to pay for the equipment. He told me that the league certainly had enough extra equipment around, and if mine was not located by the next game, we could share with his team.

Any other day, at any other time, this voice of under-standing might have touched me differently, but because of the stress of the day, Jim's response seemed so incredible. I was being treated with genuine positive regard. It felt so good!

I hung up the phone feeling as if the world had been lifted from my shoulders. My heart soared at this small example of genuine care and understanding. At the church during those days, all I experienced was attack after attack. Here was a man, probably an unbeliever in the church's eyes, giving me a break. Once again I felt the kind of love I know God has for us. Once again, I latched on to faith that Jesus loves me like that. I felt my sense of His love being renewed. Didn't Jesus say that even a cup of cold water given to one in need would be remembered?

"Blessed are the merciful, for they shall receive mercy," Jesus said in Matthew 5:7 (NASB).

Oops! I immediately headed into Karen's bedroom and sat down beside her on the bed. Tears were quietly falling down her face. I apologized to her and began to assure her that the situation had not been her fault. I began to show her the kind of understanding that I had just been shown by Jim. And as I did, I again felt the unmistakable presence of the One that I had sensed that night at Teen Challenge. I was in the presence of truth and reality again. Jesus and His love were very real to me in those few moments. In fact, it was a needed touch of Magic. I thought, "What if our lives could be like that? What if I could experience love and understanding from God and from other people, and then take that and pass it on to others?" I realized I was right on target that day. That is what God is really like.

The Father's Gift

There is a very special verse in the Old Testament where God demonstrates to us the kind of blessing He has in mind for His people. One might recognize this verse largely because it is used often as a benediction.

This God who is Love tells Moses to speak the following words, recorded in the book of Numbers, to the people. In essence, God is telling Moses, "You tell the people how good I want to be to them. If you say this blessing over them, then I'll do it!"

Take a look at the words God wanted Moses to proclaim:

> Then the Lord spoke to Moses, saying, "Speak to Aaron and to his sons saying, 'Thus shall you bless the sons of Israel. You shall say to them: The Lord bless you, and keep you; The Lord make his face shine on you, and be gracious to you; The Lord lift up His countenance on you and give you peace.'

So shall they invoke my Name on the sons of Israel and then I will bless them." (Numbers 6:22-27 NASB)

Aaron's benediction illustrates the kind of grace God wants His children to experience. He wants His people to know that He is there, to know the radiance of His presence, to know that He is watching over them and to know and experience His peace. This is the Magic, and it is deeper and stronger than any magic on Christmas morning or at Disney World.

What healing and renewal this very painful period of searching has brought into my life as I have rediscovered this great truth! The problems did not go away. But I never again doubted that God is Love, that His love is unconditional and that He holds me and all of His children in the highest regard.

And the wonder of who God is has become so much more than theory. I experienced it! It is awesome.

CHAPTER SIX

Love and Self-Worth

Has Anyone Seen My Self-Esteem?

Having grown up in a setting where my self-concept was continually nourished by love, I was almost blown away by the damage to my self-esteem as I experienced a long period of rejection by my wife and many people in my church. At the same time, I was somewhat unaware of how much damage was actually being done, because I did not realize how vital self-esteem is. God gave me some help through a very different source.

I entered the master's degree program for counseling at the State University of New York at Brockport, even as more and more difficulties were emerging in my life. On one level, I really enjoyed the counseling aspects of the ministry and wanted to learn to be more effective. On another level, I wanted some backup in terms of career options in case things got worse. It proved to be a time of wonderful learning and insight.

As I began through my studies there to realize how a person's whole being is shaped by their self-concept, I saw that I was so dependent on what other people thought of me that I had given away the control of my own self-esteem. I was trying to please everyone because I wanted them to like me, which would preserve my self-esteem. There were many problems in my marriage, but they were all aggravated by the fact that I needed my wife to give me a lot of affirmation. At that point, she could not, because she was struggling with her own needs.

I had made myself totally vulnerable by placing my sense of value into the hands of others. My self-esteem was now crashing down around me.

The second insight I had was tremendous: I saw that I could change this. I could begin to take back control of my life by looking within rather than totally outside for affirmation. And as a Christian, that would mean much more than just trying to do it myself. God holds me in the highest possible regard. I could start listening to Him!

And as I did, more Magic emerged. Much has been said and written regarding self-esteem, but we have not even begun to scratch the surface compared to what Jesus of Nazareth had to say about it.

"Are you not worth much more than they?" Jesus asked as He emphasized our worth (see Matthew 10:31).

I have struggled a great deal with my own self-esteem. What do you think of yourself? How much are you worth to God? I found the Bible to be rich with answers to these questions.

The psalmist probed for the answer in Psalm 8:

When I consider Thy heavens, the work of Thy fingers, the moon and the stars which Thou has ordained: What is man that Thou dost take thought of him? And the son of man that Thou dost care for him? (Psalm 8:3-4 NASB)

Have we not all felt this way at one time or another? Earth is just a tiny speck of dirt floating through a seemingly infinite space, and we are one person among billions. Why would God possibly care?

In the film *Rebel Without a Cause*, there is a scene in which a group of street-tough teenagers are taken on a school field trip to a planetarium. During the presentations, they are continually cutting up, seeing who can make the best wisecrack as they stare up at the universe depicted above them. They make it clear that they are too cool to care about anything. At the very end of the presentation, our solar system is destroyed as our sun explodes and lights up the entire room. As the light finally fades, the earth is gone. The rest of the universe is still there, but you cannot even tell where earth was or that it ever existed. As the speaker points out that earth will not be missed, a change comes over the faces of even these hardened young people. You see in their eyes a fear and terrible realization that the earth is, and thus they are, extremely insignificant.

But the psalmist did not stop with the vastness of the universe. He understood something of vital importance: the dignity of man!

Yet Thou has made him a little lower than God and dost crown him with glory and majesty. Thou dost make him to rule over the works of Thy hands. Thou has put all things under his feet (Psalm 8:5-6 NASB)

This is the dignity and the destiny of my fellow man and me! Do you realize that God has created you for glory and honor? The Bible says that even while you were still in the womb, God was there:

89

For Thou didst form my inward parts; Thou didst weave me in my mother's womb (Psalm 139:13 NASB)

Jesus, in the Sermon on the Mount and throughout His life and ministry, was trying to get the people to see how infinitely valuable their lives were. Every hair is numbered! If God could feed the sparrows and clothe the lilies, is He not going to take care of our needs? Are we not worth much more than they?

Jesus pointed out that God sees even a little sparrow who alights on the ground. Jesus wants us to see how loved we are by our Father. God wants to dispel our fears and to help us to see our glory as God's children.

What is the greatest truth that a person can discover? What is the most important fact that anyone can begin to comprehend? It is how valuable he or she is as a person. You are of such worth that God gave His most precious possession to win your love and trust.

For God so loved the world that He gave His only begotten Son." (John 3:16 NASB)

You are a precious, prized, and beloved person. We have sacred dignity and worth. Do you see why the multitudes were astounded at what He taught? Do you see that if my heritage is to be a dignified child of the living God, then I am indeed a fool to build my house on the sand?

I have struggled with how God sees me and what He wants from me. If you could picture Jesus before you right now, what would He say to you? Maybe not what you would expect.

There is a bumper sticker that reads, "Jesus is coming again—and boy, is he pissed!" Immediately, I was offended, but then I realized that many relate to God in this way. As I thought more about it, I wanted to somehow communicate to others that God is not like that. If you believe that Jesus would tell you what a sinner you are, you're probably wrong unless He has changed. In the Gospels, there is no record that Christ called any individual a sinner. He came to build not tear down.

To wishy-washy Peter, Jesus said, "You are a rock." To the tentative disciples Jesus said, "You are the salt of the earth, the light of the world." To a small group of uneducated fishermen, he said, "I will make you fishers of men." To money-grabbing Levi, he said, "Follow me." To Zaccheus, he said, "You are so important and of such worth that I'm eating at your house today."

Through the Gospels I see a Jesus who loved people. What would He say to you today? I believe the same message would emanate. I believe He would communicate that you are precious to Him. He would let you know that He has great dreams for you. He sees glory in your life beyond your hopes. He wants you to be able to declare with the apostle John, "And we have come to know and have believed the love which God has for us" (1 John 4:16 NASB). I believe with all my heart that He would want you to know that He thinks you are the greatest thing going.

But what about sin? Are we not sinners? Were not all people sinners? Of course, but Jesus did not tear people down by reminding them; they knew. After seeing a demonstration of His power and care, Peter fell at His feet and said, "Depart from me, for I am a sinful man." When we taste of this unconditional love and acceptance, we will be more aware of sin than ever before.

But the problem with sin is not that it breaks God's rules, but rather that it breaks God's dreams for us. He calls us to live beautiful, majestic, humble, and glorious lives for Him.

> For all have sinned and fall short of the glory of
> God. (Rom. 3:23 NASB)

The glory and joy of God is to see His children living as sons and daughters of their magnificent Father. Turning away from sin in true repentance is not an act of self- degradation; it is to see that I'm too valuable to be living in this sinful way. The prodigal son came to his senses, realized who he was and what his destiny was, and went home.

What a challenge to believe it! Can you believe that God adores you and thinks you are the greatest? His Word declares that we are more precious to Him than our own loved ones are to us.

> Consider the ravens, for they neither sow nor reap;
> and yet God feeds them; how much more valuable
> you are than the birds! (Luke 12:24 NASB)

At the conclusion of what we know as the Sermon on the Mount, Matthew tells us the "the multitudes were amazed at His teachings." They were so astounded they stood "outside of themselves." What had Jesus conveyed that was so new, so revolutionary?

Two things:

First, He had declared to them that God is a heavenly Father of love who knows each and every one of them. Second, He taught them about the extreme value of and worth of each person. The fact is, this is what He was always communicating.

Jesus loved people and always had time for them. He was constantly building people up and giving them a sense of what they could be. They have a heavenly Father who loves them and values them highly, and they can call Him their own Father. He made them feel like they were *somebody*. Little wonder that when He came down from the mountain after teaching this news that "great multitudes followed Him." Wouldn't you? Those times I have felt alone and empty and felt like a failure—He has been the one to continually say "I love you, I know the hurt, I'm here, I care, and you are still of value."

I believe that in this astounding message Jesus was reaching out to us at our deepest level of need: the need to be somebody, to matter to someone, the need for self-esteem. And who better to recognize and speak to that need? He is the Creator.

As I was trying to deal with change and hurt in my own life, I began to experience the pain and fear of losing my own sense of esteem and worth. I had been pastoring that community church for more than twelve years. Despite genuine efforts on both of our parts to save our marriage, my wife and I were divorcing, and I was leaving active ministry.

As people began turning away from me, I felt the pain of wondering if anyone really cared about me now that I was no longer fitting in to the image of a pastor, nor was I doing what was expected of me. I found my self-worth drained away. I came to feel that nothing is as valuable as a person's self-esteem. Nothing else will produce the joy-filled people that the Sermon on the Mount describes. Jesus spoke to this issue in no uncertain terms.

One day a man named Zaccheus discovered this for himself. He lived in the town of Jericho. We have every reason to suspect that he was a lonely man and might have struggled with how he felt about himself. He was a Roman tax-gatherer, which meant he was despised by his neighbors as one who had sold out to the Romans. He made his living, and a very profitable one at that, by collecting taxes for the Romans from his own countrymen. Some would get wealthy by overcharging and pocketing the difference.

Zaccheus had, however, heard something that caused him to want to see Jesus. Jesus was coming along the road to Jericho. Zaccheus could not see because of the crowd and because he was extremely small in stature. He ran ahead and climbed up a tree so that he could see Jesus.

Jesus and His disciples were moving along toward Zaccheus. He would get a good look. Then, Jesus stopped and looked up at him.

What if you were in Zaccheus' place? What would you be expecting? How does Jesus feel about you? Would He put you down? Would He point out all your sins and failures? Most of Zaccheus' neighbors thought Jesus should do that to him. They saw Zaccheus as a sinner. How would Jesus deal with you if you were in that tree?

What did Jesus do with this man who was looked upon by his peers as a traitor and sinner? Jesus tells Zaccheus, of all people, that he is so important and worthy that He wants to eat at his house that very day! What an honor! The people in the crowd grumbled to each other about how horrible it was for Jesus to go and dine with such a sinner— because in that culture, to dine with someone was to show honor and respect.

How does Zaccheus respond? He rejoices! Why? Because he was being accepted, loved, and honored by the most loving person he had ever encountered in his life. Jesus had not told him how bad he was; He had shown him respect and given him great dignity in front of the crowd that had always despised him. And they did not like it. They complained bitterly. Why didn't Jesus let Zaccheus have it for being so selfish, for being such a sinner? But you see, that is not what Zaccheus needed, and Jesus did not approach people that way.

Jesus came, in His own words, "to seek and to save that which was lost" (Luke 19:10 NASB). He came to pour acceptance and unconditional love upon fearful, suspicious human beings and to cause them to discover not only who He is but also who they are. The result is transformed lives.

What was Zaccheus' response to this love? Did he feel his sins were justified now that Jesus had shown him such love? Of course not. The Bible tells us that Zaccheus said to Jesus, "Behold, Lord half of my possessions I will give to the poor, and if I have defrauded anyone of anything, I will give back four times as much" (Luke 19:8 NASB).

What a change! He was a new man, transformed by unconditional love and acceptance, and now he wants with all his heart (and wealth) to live as a loving, caring, and Christlike child of God. His encounter with Jesus had transformed the way he saw God and himself. And Jesus then says, "Today salvation has come to this house." Why? "Because he too is a son of Abraham" (Luke 19:9 NASB). Zaccheus discovered that he was one of God's own children.

Jesus is as concerned about you as He was about Zaccheus. Jesus is concerned about the happiness of others. In His astounding Sermon on the Mount, He speaks about happiness over and over again. The happiness He speaks of is a rich, solid, joy-filled happiness—Magic!

To personally know our Father which art in heaven is to know reality as no scientist or philosopher can ever know it. There is a purpose for man's existence. We were created for a reason—to be children in a love relationship with the living God.

But it is not just reality on the grand scale of man's existence that this teaching gives us. It touches the very core of our personal identity and reason for existing. God, the Creator, is my Father, my Papa. I am never alone—I am here as part of His plan, His creation. I can be sure that I am not here merely to be part of the scenery. There is purpose for my life. No one else is like me. No one else can do what God wants me to do. The call of God is upon every single life today. As Francis Schaeffer titled one of his sermons, "There Are No Little People"—you are significant. A loving Father does not see some of His children as important and others as just existing. How many would decry that sort of parenting? God loves you and values you as much as He did Moses or David (or Hitler?). In fact, you are as dear to God the Father as is Jesus Christ. God is our heavenly Father. Do you see the awesome significance of your existence? God is intimately acquainted with you. He knows your needs even before you ask Him to fill those needs. He has a plan and a purpose for you here and now on planet earth. What will be your response to Him?

This truth began to impact my self-esteem and self-concept. We will not know Magic in our lives if our self-concept tells us we are not worthy of Magic.

Where did I obtain my self-concept? Can I do anything about changing it?

Self-concept might be defined as how you see yourself and how you see yourself in relationship to others. We have been talking about Jesus' assertion that we are valued and loved. How has that idea been striking you? If you are like most people, it goes down much easier intellectually than emotionally. Why is that?

Our self-concept is formed by a vast multitude of messages given to us from the very beginning of our lives. These messages were coming from all of the "others" who were part of our environment.

Harry S. Sullivan talked about the people in our lives that he termed "significant others." These are the people whose messages have power and influence over us. For most of us, our parents and close family members were the first significant others. We took what they said as true, whether it was or not, and whether it was healthy or not. Our self-concept was significantly shaped by those early messages.

Therefore, many of us find it very difficult to see ourselves as lovable and valuable. If the early messages from those significant others were mixed or negative, our self-concept is affected. As a child, we accepted those early messages and now find it difficult to feel otherwise. If, on the other hand, we were fortunate enough to grow in an early environment where we were loved and valued, if that was the message, we will find it much easier to embrace the idea that God is Love and that we are lovable and worthy. I am so grateful to my parents for that.

Some experts feel that our self-concept is set by the age of two. Others look at age five as the last year for any great changes. Whether or not these views are totally correct, the evidence for the importance of these early years is overwhelming. Our self-concept is extremely difficult to change.

So what good does it do to look at God's love, my worth, or even the discovery of what God wants from me if I cannot really change anyway?

It is here that we must look at how people change.

I have emphasized that the central message of the Sermon on the Mount is the priceless value of every person. I have pointed out how Jesus was constantly giving that message, how He encouraged people to see their own dignity and worth; that we are to be beautiful, loving, and faith-filled children of our heavenly Father. Within each of us is a strong desire for self-esteem, a longing to feel that we are somebody and that our life counts. We have been created to live as children of God, in His image, to glorify Him in our lives.

But we are separated from God. Man lives in guilt, fear, sin, and suspicion. Instead of being alive to God and His love, we are spiritually dead. We are, in fact, very poor in spirit.

The gospel is a transforming message; people are changed. In the Sermon on the Mount Jesus is calling upon people to be radically changed.

What takes place when people change?

First, a person's attitude may change. An attitude is a person's tendency to respond in a certain way; a person's attitude influences his opinions.

Second, a person's values may change. Values are a wider application of a group of attitudes about something. The person will probably have stronger feelings about this wider encompassing opinion.

Third, a person's behavior may change. Behavior is how a person responds to certain situations and certain stimuli.

Fourth, a person's role may change. A role is made up of the norms of behavior that the person and others expect in a given social relation. Examples would be the norms we expect of a parent, spouse, or teacher.

Fifth, a person's self-concept may change. Self-concept is how a person sees himself and how he sees himself in relationship to significant others, one of whom is God.

Now it is interesting to see that these five areas (although not a definitive list—just chosen for discussion) actually are layers of defense against change. It is a vital part of how God has created us. Otherwise, every television commercial, every friend's opinion, every authoritative statement would have us whirling to and fro, like a leaf in the wind.

It is important that these five areas maintain a sense of equilibrium, that in a sense, all five wheels are heading in the same direction. When one or more of the five elements change, there will be pressure on the others to adjust and to restore the singleness of direction once again.

These five areas, however, are not all equal; the easiest wheel to turn is an attitude. Next come values, behavior, and roles, and then by far the hardest wheel of all to turn is self-concept. A reverse effect is also important. A change in self-concept will exert great pressure on the other four wheels to adjust and move in that new direction. A change in attitude, however, will place little force upon the higher wheels and may prove to be a very short-lived change as the rest of the system will bring it back into line.

As a man thinketh in his heart, so is he. (Proverbs 23:7 KJV)

Again, I would point out that the self-concept, that sense of esteem and worth that Jesus emphasized, is so important. But it is also the most "fixed" of all the areas. As stated earlier, some psychologists believe that self-esteem is set in concrete at a very early age. Then how will people change? How can people who do not know how to love, do not know that they are loved, do not see that they have any value, learn to change? There is only one way.

A couple of years ago I was listening to a lecture by Dr. Jeremiah Donigian, a professor at Brockport, on the process of change. He talked about the defenses of the various layers just mentioned, and he emphasized that as a counselor he does not see his role as trying to change the self-concept. A counselor's goal is to help people with problems of attitude, values, behavior and sometimes even role adjustments. He pointed out to the class the tremendous pressure it takes to get through all the defenses to the self-concept. He kept underscoring how much pressure it takes and said that those who want to be "self-concept" counselors are setting an almost impossible goal.

Two lights went on inside of me. Once again, I saw secular humanism undressed. If, in fact, the self-concept must change in order for real change to take place, and it must, and if that is almost impossible to do, and it is, then we are reduced to doing a little cleaning up and applying a few Band-Aids in the areas of attitudes and values.

I also saw that this professor was describing, in a practical and beautiful way, the work of the Holy Spirit in an individual's life! For the Spirit of God can and does bring exactly the kind of pressure he said would be needed in order to get to the heart of a person, or the self-concept. The Holy Spirit alone can make us aware of the unconditional love

99

of Jesus Christ. It was so exciting for me to see that just as in philosophy, so also here in psychology the Bible has the answers, and it even helps to make the questions clearer. Can a person change? Can his self-concept be radically changed? The answer is *yes*. He can allow the most loving of all significant others to come into his life!

The apostles wrote about this change:

Therefore, if anyone is in Christ, he is a new creation; the old has gone, the new has come! (2 Corinthians 5:17 NIV)

Because the love of God has been poured out within our hearts through the Holy Spirit who was given to us. (Romans 5:5 NASB)

Do not marvel that I have said to you, you must be born again. (John 3:7 NASB)

I hope this helps us to see why it is so important to reach out to Jesus. Without coming to the person who is Love, we will be doomed even with the best of intentions to adjusting an attitude here, a behavior there. We will not become new creations in Christ. It is not just deciding to be moral; it is not just deciding that Jesus is OK; it is inviting Jesus the Lord and Savior to come to dwell in our innermost being. When that happens, then inevitably the other areas of values and behavior will be changed, but not by human effort. Rather, we come to know and believe the love God has for us, to realize our value. Then we will be made new from the inside out.

Stop a minute and think of a time in your life you felt very loved. Isn't it something to realize that God has loved you that much and even more each moment of your life? As I think of those moments in my life when I have felt very loved by God or by another person, I now realize that God loves me that much constantly!

As many of us struggle with our self-concept, how we need to know this unconditional love. Perhaps the early messages of our life convinced us that significant others will love us only when we perform or achieve or obey or give in. Perhaps the early message was that we are just not lovable.

Whatever the message, Jesus, *the* significant other, declares His unconditional love for me—just as I am.

Give yourself permission to drink in that message. Open your heart to this love. Let this one who is Love, love you.

Through the things I was learning in the master's program and through looking at the teachings of Jesus, my self-esteem was being renewed. I did start to take more control of my life. With a renewed commitment to the Lord and a new understanding of myself, I was moving toward growth.

Despite my situation, God is Love.

And something that had been obvious all along really began to crystallize: If God holds me in such loving high regard, then who are you? It is obvious, and yet if we do not stop to consider its implications, it is so "obvious" that it has no impact upon us.

We are all God's kids!

Look at this genealogy found in Luke's story about Jesus:

The son of Cainan, the son of Arphaxed, the son of Shem, the son of Noah, the son of Enoch, the son of Jared, the son of Mahalaleel, the son of Cainan, the son of Enosh, the son of Seth, the son of Adam, the son of God. (Luke 4:36-38 NIV)

Most of us from a Christian background think of the genealogy as tracing our ancestry to Adam. But Adam is not my ancestral father—nor yours.

Luke takes me all the way back to my true Father: "...the son of Seth, the son of Adam, the son of God..."

God is my Father.

We are not talking about an ambiguous sort of brotherhood among mankind. God really truly is my Father...*and yours.*

We are all God's kids!

Take a moment to think about some of those kids:

...some you know and love,

...some make you uneasy,

...some are rich,

...some are happy,

...some are starving,

...some are dying,

...some of them you fear,

...some perhaps make you angry,

...some you care about, some you do not,

...some you perhaps avoid, dislike, or even hate.

Every human being you can picture in your mind is one of your Father's kids!

No wonder God keeps telling me to love others!

Now it made more sense; it was not just obvious, it made sense. Why does Jesus command me to love you? Why does Peter tell me to love you with all my strength? Why does Paul say to love more and more and more? Why does John say that if I do not love you, then to say I love God is a lie?

Because of *who you are*!

How blind we are! How could we ever do the things we do to one another if we really saw this as true? We ignore or even butcher our own brothers and sisters.

As I thought about this, I thought about my own three children. No wonder God gets angry with us. What if day after day you came to me and told me how much you love and respect me? I would be thrilled. It would be wonderful to hear you say it.

But I also learn that you are terrible to my children. You ignore them, you cheat them, you gossip about them, you even hurt them. Yet daily you keep coming to tell me how much you love and respect me. You know that I will quickly tire of hearing your words. We will soon be discussing your treatment of my kids.

We have to look at how often we have treated God exactly that way! How often we have declared in church, or in prayer, our love for God and in the same hour have ignored or even hurt one of His kids.

If we are going to please God and bring joy to His heart, then we must come to grips with this obvious and profound truth: We are His kids—all of us.

One practical place I applied this was at my job. I worked at a counseling facility and saw a large number of clients each week. I enjoyed what I did and usually had no problem with my sessions. Sometimes, however, I felt drained or down and would rather be somewhere else.

When this happens, I take a moment and remind myself that this next person I am going to counsel is not just another person with a problem. This is a very special person—one of my Father's children. That client is a valuable and important person.

It works! It turns what looks like a burden into an opportunity. With that perspective, every hour of the day we have a chance to live among precious and significant people. That perspective removes boredom and brings excitement into everyday living.

I choose to have that perspective. I choose to see life as an exciting opportunity to help others and myself toward our destiny as God's dearly loved children!

As my own self-esteem was being renewed, my life was not getting any easier. As I started to take back control of my life and stand more strongly for what I believed, others became more convinced I was not what they wanted in a minister. I do not know how I would have survived those days had I not come to see how much God loved me and how valuable and precious I was to Him. It gave me a hope to cling to through the storms.

Ultimately I even let go of Him. He, however, never let go of me.

CHAPTER SEVEN

Loving Redemption

I Find Out He Means It

The day had finally arrived for me to leave the church I had pastored for almost thirteen years. I remember very little about that final Sunday—I know I simply conducted the service as if it were any other Sunday. I had done all the hurting I wanted to do and just wanted to wrap it up. It was the first time in my life that I had no idea of what the future held. Every door seemed closed. Some of the people were heartbroken that I was giving up. It was also the same time in which Sharon and I had to leave our home and move into an apartment until we could move into the house we were renting. What a week.

Where was this God of love? I do not believe that at that point I was even asking the question. I did not realize that He was going to answer me anyway!

Some may find this hard to understand, but through all of this, Sharon and I remained good friends. We still are today. When she saw how the church had treated me and pretty much forced me to resign, she stuck with me for a while. Once again the marriage issues were put on hold.

This had been the worst phase of my life. I was without a job, had a wife who would have left if it was totally up to her, and knew that I had failed God. Also, I was distancing myself from a God who had let my world fall apart when I had sincerely repented several years before. I saw no hope, no way out, and felt totally trapped in a terrible situation.

But God is Love, and God is never finished.

I received a call asking me if I would consider becoming an interim assistant minister at Parkminster Presbyterian Church, located just west of Rochester. It was about ten times the size of Ridgeland. It was not what I wanted to do. I was finishing my master's degree in counseling and wanted to find a counseling position. Nothing materialized, and I finally accepted the opportunity at Parkminster. Thank You, Lord.

The year that I served there turned out to be wonderful. The people responded to my ministry in a very positive way. They seemed hungry to hear of the love of God. Like Ridgeland, they had been through some very difficult times. The pastor and his wife, Ev and Nancy Sahrbeck, were terrific to me.

I remember the tremendous anxiety I felt on the day I finally had to tell Ev that Sharon and I were separating. I feared his response. At Ridgeland, I had been asked to step down because we were having problems, let alone this. He did not judge, he did not attack. He responded with incredible love and care. In fact, he made me feel as if I was still very much needed at the church. I was stunned. Ev's unconditional love on that morning is one of the main reasons I am still a Christian.

I experienced a great deal of healing in my life. Even when they realized what was happening between Sharon and me, the people in the church continued to be loving and supportive. Rather than condemning, one dear Christian lady said, "No wonder your ministry to us was effective. You were ministering out of your own hurt."

Finally, Sharon and I reached a place of decision—our marriage was over. She no longer wanted to live in misery for a mistake she made at the age of nineteen, and I did not want to spend the rest of my life with someone who did not want to be with me. I stopped manipulating and controlling, and I let it go. The strain on us and our three children had just become too damaging. I never, ever, would have believed it, but I was getting divorced. I did not believe in divorce, but I was doing it—another horrible failure. And my time at Parkminster was drawing to a close with the arrival of the new senior minister.

No marriage, no job, no home (we had lost our house), no ministry—a dead end.

Often through the years of my ministry people would say that I could not really understand because I had never been in their place. Intellectually I would acknowledge that, but inside I thought there was no one that I could not relate to; they were just looking for an excuse. How wrong I was; how I have learned.

You just do not understand the pain and the rejection and the sense of failure until you have been there. I was too quick to condemn, too quick to judge, too quick to write people off as having disobeyed God. I am not advocating that we condone divorce, but dear God, we need to be so much more understanding and supportive and redemptive.

And I was also surprised by the pain of my job loss. Now, working with people in that situation, I understand it. Now I know about the devastating loss of self-esteem, the anxiety of having control of your life taken away, and the cold fear of not being able to find another job. Again, unless you have been there.

What now? What next? Where to?

Fortunately, God is who I had thought He is. To my total amazement, over the next few years He restored everything I thought I had lost forever.

The first time I saw her was on a warm, sunny day in late June. I had been the pastor of Ridgeland for eight years, and Sharon was running a terrific daycare center at the church. Patty had come to work at the daycare.

I do not remember exactly, but I am sure I was impressed by how very pretty she was. I got to know her a little as the summer went by. I was in the midst of some of the more difficult days of my marriage. I had no idea that during that summer she had developed a tremendous crush on me. I am so very grateful that I did not know that. That's all I would have needed at that time.

Patty left at the end of the summer but came back to work there again two years later. This time we developed more of a friendship, but I still did not have a clue as to her feelings. Again, I am grateful. After about a year, she left the daycare again.

Then, about three years later our paths crossed one more time. At that time, I knew that my marriage was over. Sharon and I were separating. Karen was playing Pony League baseball, and Patty had started to come to some of her games. (I thought she was coming to watch baseball.)

Then on the night of the final game of the season, Patty, knowing it could be the last time we would see each other, invited herself over. I had no idea what she was up to.

The months preceding this night had left me feeling very unloved and unlovable. I was absolutely and totally astounded as this beautiful young woman told me how much she loved me, how much she had loved me since that very first summer. OK, so I am a trained counselor. Yes, I know how totally vulnerable I was. Yes, I should have used my great knowledge about these things, but I never had a chance. I was totally blown away. I did not even think yet about whether I loved her. (I was very attracted to her.) I was in awe of the fact that somebody like her loved me—me, who had heard the exact opposite for years. I behaved myself that night, but my mind and heart were becoming filled with a hope for something that I thought was gone forever.

Over the next several months it became clear that she really did love me. She was there to listen and to care. Soon, the love was mutual (although to this day she insists that she loves me more). It was a total turnaround. I had gone from a relationship where no matter what I did, Sharon could not love me, to one where no matter what I did, I was loved. It was astounding!

Next came the issue of my career. This was a struggle. I was just finishing up my master's when my time at Parkminster came to a close. Now, I truly had no job, no idea of what to do.

I tried to get my own counseling practice started, but it just did not take off. Finally, I was hired as a counselor at a live-in facility for emotionally disturbed teenagers. It was not a good fit. I wanted to do counseling, and they wanted more of an enforcer. After a few months they realized that I was not what they needed, and they let me go. I was a little upset but not much. I liked many of the kids, but I was not that sorry to leave the environment. And besides, I had a hunch that the Lord might be up to something.

I had applied for a counseling position at the Women's Career Center in Rochester several months earlier. When I called, I was informed that the positions were all filled. Shortly after that, I took the position at the live-in center. The very week that they let me go I received a phone call from Laurie Kaiser, the director of counseling at the Women's Career Center, inviting me in for an interview. So, as I sat there learning that I was being let go, I actually would be having a job interview the next day for something I wanted much more.

After several interviews, I was offered the new position. Real counseling, much better hours, and almost twice as much money. The Lord had now opened the door for me to do what I had hoped to do. I loved the job, the people, and the challenges for the twelve-plus years I was there.

And still, He was not through. Sharon and I had lost our house through some difficult financial circumstances. So, when the marriage ended, our three children and I had nowhere to live. God met that need. First, Patty's mom and step-father offered to let us stay in their house while they were in Florida for the winter.

Patty had money available from an inheritance from her father, who had died the year before. Sharon helped us to find a home in the area where we wanted to live. (I told you she was an excellent real estate agent and still a friend.)

My relationship with Patty continued to flourish. Our love for one another continued to grow. I teased her about not knowing whether she was a devil or an angel; it all happened pretty fast. Was the god of Eros winning, or was this a blessed gift from the true God? As time went by it became very clear that our love was a wonderful, precious gift of God, just as she was.

We were married, and I found myself in the kind of marriage my heart had longed for since my teen years. It would have been quite easy to assume my quest was over and let that "love of my life" take first place as my source of joy and happiness. But Patty knew better; she knew how important my faith was to me, and she also had her own incredible hunger for God. She did not allow me to settle for Eros.

Patty gently and firmly pushed me back into the life of a church. We started to attend Raymond Memorial Baptist Church. I had known Bill Kerr, the pastor, for many years. There we discovered a loving and healing fellowship.

A home, a marriage, a wonderful job, a great church home—all of this restored. Did I deserve it? Of course not, but

God truly is the Father of the prodigal son. I know that is who He is and what He is like. I believe it with all of my heart.

I was well on my way to being "back" with God, although older and much, much wiser. Paul Garlinton, for years one of my closest friends in the ministry, said a very special thing to me one afternoon when I opened up to him about how much I had failed.

"John," he said, "you needed this. You needed to know that you are human; now you can begin to minister to humans." Knowing that I was still feeling like quite a failure, he went on to say that he would be very pleased to have me on his ministerial staff any day. It was a gift of love that Paul gave me that afternoon.

There were still two more milestones on my journey back. The first was quite traumatic; the second would not seem very momentous to anyone but me.

What brought about the trauma was an event in the life of my oldest daughter, Karen. Patty and I had been married for about two years; all three of the children had been living with us. Things had been going well, though I was still not very involved with the church.

I will not here give the details of what happened; that is Karen's story, not mine. But I will say it brought up all the old feelings once again. Was God (Tash) after me again? Was I to be seen once more as a failure? This was hitting me very hard.

This time, however, I turned to God rather than away! Patty and I had gone to her grandfather's summer home on Canandaigua Lake to spend the weekend. It was July. There is a couch in front of one of the windows that gives a clear view of that beautiful lake. I sat alone on that couch early on a beautiful sunny morning talking to Him.

The barriers of many difficult years came crashing down. I turned back to Him like a child. We talked about what I was feeling, my fears, my hurt, my sin, and my need. I committed the whole situation to Him and completely opened up my heart and life to Him again. Never again have I held Him at arm's length.

The problem did not immediately clear up, because it could not. But I felt a peace and assurance that went way beyond the circumstances. And I also received some clear direction from my Lord, who told me to love and care for her in the same way that He loved me and to leave the rest up to Him. And I did. And He was faithful.

Finally, the barriers were down; God and I were best friends again.

The much less traumatic event took place one morning as I was driving to work. I was listening to a tape of sermons that I had given fifteen years earlier while I was the pastor of Ridgeland Community Church. It was during the period of time when I first began to fear that the church was turning away from the love message I had discovered. I spoke with passion, assurance, and sincerity. I spoke of a way of living that could produce all of the things my heart longs for: peace, reality, meaning, fulfillment.

The tape had come into my hands in a very roundabout but providential way. That sermon was a summary of what I had been trying to impart to that congregation. A very dear family, the Bells, had left the church upon moving to Dallas. I sent them a tape of the sermon because I felt they would be interested in that which I was finding exciting. Then twelve years later they moved back to Rochester and began attending our new church in Fairport. A few nights before, their son Chris had given me a copy of that very tape.

It felt very strange to be listening to myself preaching fifteen years earlier. As I listened, I knew that God was giving me another chance to hear, another chance to catch a vision that had so excited me back then. Tears came to my eyes—tears of regret, tears of hope—and a new commitment to share this message in any way God chose. I realized that in a new way I was once again serving Him.

And yet, there was more—an area too painful for me to touch, to even acknowledge. But this God of incredible love moved into even that.

On a Sunday afternoon in the spring of 1992, I was sitting at the dinner table with Patty, Karen, and her boyfriend, Ray. He had just asked me for permission to become engaged to Karen. I was delighted. This was such a wonderful fulfillment of that morning I had turned back to God and turned Karen over to Him. Since then, she had found a renewed and vibrant faith in the Lord. She had grown so much, and now God had brought her into a loving relationship with a wonderful, loving, spiritual partner.

Who could have ever guessed that one day a young man who was helped by the very Teen Challenge Center I had started more than twenty years earlier would be asking for my daughter's hand? Ray is a young man who clearly loves the Lord. Jesus has set him free and saved his life, and Ray would share that with anyone who would listen.

In the middle of this moment, the phone rang. I was totally stunned as the gentleman on the other end of the line told me that he was a police detective who was about to place my seventeen-year-old daughter under arrest for felony assault. Nothing could have prepared me for this moment. I was in shock.

This is about the deep Magic of God's love, the Magic that is at work in the dark and desperate times of our lives when it feels like we are being overwhelmed and torn apart. Right now, there would be no simple, magic answer.

Over the previous two years, Kathy had drifted further and further from us. She did not want to be told what to do; she did not feel that she needed to answer to us about where she was or what she was doing. Over time, we frankly and sadly allowed her to wear us down. We did not approve of many of the people she was hanging out with; we were concerned about where she was and how she was coming home later and later at night.

I once had been quick to judge people whose teenagers would go astray. I did not understand how powerful their wills can be, how fierce their rebellion can become. In this case, Kathy had now ended up in the wrong place at the wrong time, but I also knew that she had been putting herself in the wrong places for years. Still, I would never have expected this.

The detective let me talk with her on the phone, and for the first time in over a year the blunt, hard front was gone. She was truly hurting. She had gone to the police station expecting to be answering questions, never dreaming she would be arrested. She would be spending the night in jail. She was totally out of my hands.

This had been a very difficult couple of months for us already. I had gone through minor surgery, we had faced a horrendous financial situation, and Patty had endured a crisis in her job.

Patty had been working as a customer service supervisor when suddenly her manager decided to change her hours to noon to 9 p.m. We both felt very frustrated by that change. She would not get home until almost 10 each night. She would not see Jason all week, and evening activities would be all but eliminated.

We prayed about it and realized anew that our relationship and our family were priorities before the Lord. We felt strongly that God would handle the situation if we put those things first. Patty would tell her boss those hours were unacceptable.

Those of you who have feared for your job in these days of tight job markets and downsizings will have some understanding of the anguish Patty was experiencing. We knew the Lord had opened the door to this job in the first place, but now—where are You, Lord? Where is the Magic?

She was not fired. She was, however, expected to take a demotion to a non-management job in customer service. Well, that was sort of an answer. We had put God first, and, well, Patty still had a job.

In the days ahead, many people expressed great admiration for us, and especially for Patty, for having taken such a stand. That was nice, but I could tell she was very disappointed.

One afternoon, she was taking the bull by the horns, which is definitely her style, and was typing up a resume to look for a new job. A manager from another area came by and asked her what she was doing. She told him what and why. He had an idea, and within days Patty had accepted another supervisory position in another division of the company! She was ecstatic! God had once again been faithful, and we had been able to trust Him in a way that showed we were growing.

God worked out another miracle in the financial area by leading us to some excellent professional help. I survived the surgery, which was not serious, but to me anything to do with the medical or dental area is cause for the highest level of alarm.

So, just as we seemed to be emerging from those shots, the call came about Kathy. I hung up the phone, stunned, and told Patty, Karen, and Ray what had happened. Karen already knew about it; to Ray these types of things were a "normal" part of life; and Patty felt as if God was determined to keep hammering us.

We tried to stay in the chair of faith. It was very difficult. We first had to drive to the police station to pick up Kathy's car. When we arrived, she had already been taken to the city jail, but the detective talked to us for a few minutes. He was not very encouraging; he told us we had a long road ahead of us.

My head was spinning as I drove Kathy's car home. One second I was praying, the next remembering this little girl who had been the most fun, loving, and impish of my children, the next violently attacking myself as a parent, and then questioning a God who could let such a thing happen. I fought hard to keep leaning on the Lord.

When we arrived home we felt helpless. Kathy would be arraigned the next morning. Of course, we would be there. At some point I called Sharon, but I am not sure just when it was. Then, we finally received what seemed like a touch of God's help.

Patty decided to call the man who had been her father's lawyer. She looked up his home number in the phone book. She got his answering machine and left a message. To our surprise, he called back fairly soon.

As it turned out, this was the son of her dad's lawyer, but he was, in fact, the person we needed. He was the criminal attorney in the family. As he was telling us what we needed to do, he expressed astonishment that we had been able to get him on a Sunday. "No one gets me on Sunday," he said. He was exactly the person we needed, and God had opened exactly the right door.

We called our pastor, Bill Kerr, and he was there within fifteen minutes along with another church member, Bob Longhouse. They prayed with us, and after they left all we could do was wait to see what the next morning would bring.

The deepest Magic of God's love does not work overnight. The deep Magic of God's love does not form us into new creatures in Christ instantly. That is often what we want. That is often what our culture tells us life should be like. That is why surface solutions of positive attitudes and personality styles and behavior modifications are so very popular. The deep Magic of God's love, however, is aimed at change and renewal of the heart. It works from the inside out. Its magical impact on our lives may take a lifetime. It works on what we are becoming. The Magic is an outgrowth of what is taking place inside. It is spiritual and eternal. Yeah, you knew there was a catch to all this Magic stuff.

But if there is "a catch," it is only because the deep Magic of God's love does not come cheap and easy. The deepest Magic of all time worked when God the Father allowed His only-begotten Son, Jesus, to be killed on a cross one Friday. That same Magic now is at work through the Spirit of Christ dwelling in His followers and ultimately will lead to the incredible, magical ending when we live with Him forever.

But now, we see that Magic, as Paul said, through a dark and cloudy mirror. This does not make it less real: life is still meant to be abundant and joyful, and we should rejoice in all the blessings of God in our lives. But sometimes, the mirror will be very dark and the work of Magic very deep.

In my years at Teen Challenge, there were several occasions when I stood in court with one of our young men. How could I ever have known that someday I would be doing the same thing for my own daughter?

It turned out to be a drawn-out process over several months with one court date after another. God was with us, but it did not feel very magical. Because of the fact the other girl had provoked Kathy and come at her, because she had never been in trouble before, and because the court received a great deal of positive input from some of her teachers, the charges were reduced and Kathy was placed on probation without a permanent record.

God was restoring so many wonderful things in my life. But this was one area that I felt I would always regret: Kathy. I would look at home videos of her and see the most delightful, alive, happy, and wonderful child you could imagine. I would kick myself, wondering how I had failed to fill her life with love and attention. She took the brunt of our marriage problems; she was at such a vulnerable age. She did not fall in love with baseball and other sports like Karen did.

But it was not just time and activities. She grew up during the time my life was ravaged with anxiety and uncertainty. I would look at those tapes and realize I had been so entangled in my own turmoil that I had missed out on so much with such a delightful little girl.

And I felt I would carry that regret for the rest of my life.

But God just keeps at it!

Kathy's life did not magically turn around. She continued to do her own thing. But little by little we became more a part of her life again. She went to college, graduated with a two-year degree, moved in with a guy, had a beautiful little girl, secured a good job, moved back home, moved back out, moved back home, back out, and so forth. And we started more and more to talk, to love, to see the old and real Kathy.

Then, one Father's Day she gave me a card—and in it she thanked me for all I had been to her as a father, even when she was a child. In that card she recalled special, precious times we had shared together. She pointed out specific events as highlights of her childhood. Despite my own stress and problems, she had known how much I loved her! What an incredible and special gift she is. The area I thought I would always regret and feel like a failure in has become one of the greatest joys of my life. She is such a wonderful, gifted young lady.

God is Love—Redemptive Love. The image of the prodigal's father is real. God is like that. What a miracle of redemptive love. The psalmist declares: "Taste and see that the Lord is good!" (Psalm 34:8 NASB). Oh, is He!

I did not deserve it, but God had continued to love me with an incredible, restoring, unconditional love. And so He does with you. Whoever you are, wherever you are, He is right there with that love. Waiting, like that father, to run and throw His arms of love around you the second you give Him a chance.

I needed that kind of love...and boy, did He give it! How I hope you too discover the wonder of who God is.

CHAPTER EIGHT

Three Great Discoveries

The Love Theology of the Bible

Following my time of reflection in Florida, I came back determined to recapture and live anew what I saw as the Magic of God's love. There were some key questions that needed to be answered.

First, was my quest realistic? Was I just kidding myself to think that life could be magical, with God's love as a constant reality?

Second, if it could, how was this quest going to be any different from all the other times I had tried to get started again and had stalled out? How could one keep this Magic alive?

After reviewing my walk with God, that which you have read thus far, and reflecting on much of the New Testament, I decided that my quest was not only realistic, but also what I sought was probably quite normal in New Testament Christianity. These people did not live in a Disney World; they experienced many trials and tribulations, but through it all they expressed a joy and an excitement about what they had discovered in the person of Jesus Christ that overrode any obstacles they faced, including physical death. They were so excited about what God had done for them that they went to the ends of the earth to share it. Even in prison, awaiting execution, they would sing hymns of praise to God and write about the great joy in their hearts. They also loved and encouraged one another in times of joy and times of sorrow. The pages of the Gospels and the book of Acts describe people who are living in the Magic of God's love.

I also discovered a very exciting parallel between my picture of Magic and those who heard the Sermon on the Mount. Jesus declared: "Blessed are the poor in spirit." The word He used for "blessed" was connected to a saying that described the island of Cyprus as the "blessed isle." That island had all one needed for bliss, with its climate, lushness, and beautiful sunlit beaches. That image may have come to their minds as Jesus declared that those "poor in spirit," those who recognized their need for this wonderful God and His love, would begin to know that kind of bliss—all one would need for joy could be accessed by surrendering to this loving Father.

All right, so how could I recapture it and then live in that which I was seeking? There had been many things that had helped me to know some times of Magic in my life:

Len Evans' teaching was perhaps the strongest. Books and tapes on the power of positive thinking had helped. The study of the whole area of self-esteem had helped a great deal.

Books by Francis Schaeffer that show the glorious truth of God's Word had helped.

I was in the midst of reviewing all of the above, and I was spending more time in prayer and Bible study, when light flooded my life and it all came together. The answer, of course, was Him! The person of the Magic.

About once a year, I read through the books of *The Chronicles of Narnia*. These books tell the wonderful story of children from our world visiting the land of Narnia, where they encounter many adventures and come to know the ruler of Narnia, Aslan, whom I have described earlier. I ran across a portion where Lucy encounters Aslan for the first time in quite awhile. The book mentions how her heart leaps as she hears again the voice she longs to hear above all others. It was as if a light switch had suddenly been turned on!

I cannot explain it, but in that moment as my own heart leapt, I knew that Christ Himself was the source of all I was seeking. Before that moment I knew that, but suddenly I really knew it. He is the joy, the peace, the power! He is the source of genuine self-esteem. He is the reason for all legitimate positive thinking. And He is, of course, the source of love, which is to flow through us to others.

Hundreds of times I had read Paul's description of how the rest of his life (which really was quite a fine and upstanding life) was like garbage compared to knowing Jesus Christ. In that moment, I felt I understood Paul's statement and feelings. The greatest Magic of all is the person, life, and existence of Jesus Christ, who has chosen us and invited us to be His friends.

What could give a greater sense of wonder and Magic than to realize that God was here among us? He walked on this earth, He felt joy and sorrow, He touched the lives of people all around him, and He was the most loving person who ever lived. Think of it: *He was here, and He is Love.*

Add to that the fact that He loved each and every one of us so much that He was willing to suffer and die so that we might become part of His eternal family.

And now, through the presence of His Spirit, He comes to be a part of our daily lives, living at the very center of our beings, loving and guiding us through the joys, sorrows, opportunities, challenges, and Magic of each day.

You see, the problem is not that I long to escape to the magic of a Disney World; the tragedy is that we fail to see how pale such magic is in light of what our Lord Jesus has promised to bring to us.

In Him was life and that life is the light of men (John 1:4 NIV). The foundation of all that is magical and good and positive is a personal relationship with the Lord Jesus Christ. That is the legitimate source, the true Vine.

I began to understand how it all comes together. When I first became a Christian, one thing that was very clear was the total difference between being a Christian and not being a Christian. I saw that when someone received Christ into their lives they were a new creation. They passed from death to life. Now one might not know the exact moment or even year when that happened, but it made all the difference.

I have now shared with you the journey from whence came what I call the three great discoveries. They are absolutely life-transforming. They are completely biblical. In fact, get your Bible as I now try to hammer home the missing piece to the abundant life puzzle.

The Three Great Discoveries
Discovery One: The Wonder of Who God Is

When I first became a Christian as a senior in high school, I learned the "Four Spiritual Laws" in preparation to go out and do personal evangelism. The first step was:

"God loves you and has a wonderful plan for your life."

As I recall, we would quickly go over the first step, barely acknowledging it, in our haste to get to the second step:

"You are separated from God by sin." That was the big step—giving people the "Good News" that they were sinners. A friend of mine later called it the Good News of Damnation.

Now, many years later and much more knowledgeable about the Bible, I realize that in fact that first "step" is the Good News!

God loves you, God adores you, God delights in you!

The Bible is the greatest book ever written. It is, in fact, God communicating to His children a message filled with love and hope. And, the ultimate conclusion of the Bible is "God Is Love."

1 John 4:8, 4:16	It could not be clearer God is Love. He does not just have and express love—He is Love! What is God like? What is the ultimate reality behind the universe? *Him*!
John 14:9	Again, a crystal-clear statement. As we look at the life, actions and words of Jesus of Nazareth we are seeing God. He is that gentle, that loving, that caring.
Heb. 1:3	Jesus is not just a lot like God the Father. This tells us in the original language that He is the exact image and imprint of God.
Col. 1:15	This tells us that Jesus is the exact likeness of the unseen God.
John 3:16	God loved the world. He loved you and me. He was not disgusted with us; He loves us!
Psalm 139	God knows and loves me. It is not just a general love of humanity. He has been intimately involved in your life since before you were born! He thinks lovingly of you every moment of the day. You are precious to Him.

Luke 12:6-7	He holds you in the highest regard. You are of immeasurable value to Him.
1 John 4:16	Can you believe it too? Do you know and actually believe the love God has for you?

The Son of God, Jesus of Nazareth, the carpenter, lies flat-out on the ground in a garden just outside of Jerusalem. He is in despair. He is praying to His heavenly Father to please let this cup pass from Him. He asks not once but three times. The "cup" is what is coming in the next few hours: the betrayal, the desertion, the joke of a trial, the beating, the spitting, the mockery, the execution by one of the cruelest means devised by the evil mind of man. And what we will never comprehend, the shame of bearing the sins of the world upon Himself.

The Father says no. Why, in His Son's most desperate hour, does this loving heavenly Father say no? The answer to that is the key to who God really is.

"Son, I can't. I'm sorry. I love them too much to let them go; John and Bill and Mary and Breanna...and you, dear reader."

He will move heaven and earth and a cow to bring you to Himself.

Zephaniah 3:17 says you are His delight. He rejoices and exalts over you. He sings because of you.

He was here, and He is Love!

Discovery Two: What God Really Wants from Us

Of course, I have already shared this life-transforming discovery in the pages of this book. I found it in the Word of God. It saved my world.

Many honest Christians will concede their Christian life has not been all it was cracked up to be. Where is the joy, the power, the fellowship, the reality? I believe with all my heart that this discovery is where the reality begins. It is the missing piece to the abundant life puzzle.

And it is so simple. I guess that is why so many people miss it—it's not very religious or spiritual. It is just simple and practical—like that carpenter.

If in fact God is Love, then it makes sense that the one thing He would want from me is that I give love to others, to His children!

John 13:34-35	When the One who created the heavens and the earth summarizes all of His teaching into one statement, it has got to be the key to the universe—and it is.
Romans 13:8-10	Does this one commandment really fulfill all of the law's requirements? That is what it says.
Matthew 9:13, 12:7	What does God really want from us? The sacrifices of religion or the love and compassion of Jesus?

1 Thessalonians 3:12-13; 4:9	What is true holiness? What must I do to be established in it? Notice the intensity with which Paul exhorts Christians to excel more and more and more in their love for one another.
Galatians 5:14	Again, Paul declares that this command fulfills all the others.
Ephesians 2:8-10	We are saved to do deeds of love. This tells us not only what we are saved from but what we are saved for.
Titus 2:14	God is redeeming kingdom people to do the deeds of love and giving.

It is important to realize that we do have the love to pull this off. We do not have to wait until we "feel" love. Love is a choice to decide to love others as Jesus has loved us—"to do unto others."

Romans 5:5	We do have the love to pull this off!
John 17:26	We absolutely do!

I so wish that all Christians were required to know 1 Peter 1:22 as well as they know John 3:16: "Since you were cleansed from your sins when you accepted the truth of the Good News in order that you can have sincere love for each other, see to it that you really do love each other intensely with all your hearts" (author's paraphrase).

Please memorize this verse.

Discovery Three: The Wonder of Who We Are!

As my dear friend Len Evans used to say, there is one thing to which we remain eternally blind. It is not to what Jesus had to say about God; we sort of get that. We are blind to what He had to say about who we are! We are God's children, God's kids! Really! We have incredible value and worth. We have an amazing destiny!

The genealogy of Luke (Luke 3) shows that God is my Father and yours. Why does He command me to love you? Because it's moral, because it's nice, because it will make me feel good? No. It is because of who you are: a precious, amazing wondrous prince or princess of the King of Kings!

They do not know nor do they understand: They walk about in darkness; All the foundations of the earth are shaken. I said, You are gods, and all of you are Sons of the Most High. Nevertheless, you will die like men and fall like any one of the princes. (Psalm 82:5-7 NASB).

These may be the most tragic words ever written. We were created to be children of the living God, princes and princesses of His kingdom, and instead we will die like mere men, falling so short of what our destiny was to be.

We must not let that happen! We must tell people by our words and by holding them in the highest possible regard, treating them as if we really believe in their value, that they are destined to be children of God, children of His kingdom.

How I treat the most insignificant person to cross my path is how I treat Jesus. That "little one" is that precious. (Matthew 25:31-46)

How would our world change if our eyes were opened to this truth?

When I was attending Auburn Community College in the spring of 1966, we had a weekend event that was to include a concert by Jay and the Americans. We were excited that a group with several Top 10 hits was going to be at our little school.

As we arrived that night, we were told that due to illness they were not coming. A replacement group had been sent up from New York City. The "group" turned out to be two guys. One was tall and slender; the other was a little guy playing a guitar. Instead of hearing several Top Ten hits, they sang songs written by the little guy. They did have one hit; in fact it had just sold its millionth copy that week. The hit was "Sounds of Silence" and the group was Simon & Garfunkel! We were listening to the songs that would become anthems of the 1960s and 1970s. We had no clue.

How differently we would have treated those guys that night had we any idea of their future destiny. We could have gotten autographs. We could have probably taken them out for coffee. Instead, we pretty much ignored them.

The Bible gives me more than a clue about my fellow human being. How exciting! Every day we live in a world of potential princes and princesses of the living God. No wonder Jesus kept telling us to love them!

Magic, Magic, Magic
His Magic Presence, Magic Seeds, and a Magic Mirror

Now that I had found anew the person of the Magic, I was determined not to lose that closeness again.

On the night before His death, Jesus told His disciples that He would continue to show Himself to them but not to the world.

One disciple asked Him, "Lord, how will You show yourself to us, but not the world?"

Jesus answered, "If anyone loves me, he will keep My word (i.e. The New Commandment); and My Father will love him, and we will come to him, and make our abode with him" (John 14:23 NASB).

Here He is using the imagery of the Old Testament, when the glory of God filled the tabernacle (a tent that served as their temple), and saying that we will walk in that presence when we are keeping the Word, walking in love.

There it was! This was the presence and the reality of God that I had longed for throughout my Christian life! Whenever I would endeavor to show love for others, Jesus promised to be there in a glorious and genuine way. I will be in Him, in the pulsating life of the Spirit.

This was astounding to me! I could know His presence just by treating a coworker with kindness. I could know His presence just by giving a kind word to a waitress or a gas-station attendant.

And I found it worked! I was not very good at it, but still it worked. I sensed God in my life as never before even when my attempts to love were far from perfect, far from being consistent. As I had suspected, we can have much greater Magic in our lives than that for which we so often settle.

I had found the closeness to God that I had always wanted. I did not have to wait until I was in church, I did not have to wait for an opportunity to pray at length. I just had to give out what He had given me—real love.

How do I get to know this God of wonder? Discovery Two is the key to that!

The "Secret" of Fellowship with God

People all over the world seem to be seeking God. Some anthropologists use that as a factor that makes man unique from other animals. But the psalmist declares something quite different. In Psalm 53 it says:

> The Lord has looked down from heaven upon the sons of men, To see if there are any who understand, who seek after God. They have all turned aside... there is no one who does good. (Psalm 14:2, 3 NASB)

With all of the religion going on in the world, how can he make such a statement? Because fellowship with God is not based upon religion—it is based upon how I treat you.

The psalmist then goes on to describe the fact that people are corrupt—their actions toward one another are evil. No one does "good" to another: "They devour my people as men eat bread" (Psalm 14:4 NIV).

What a contrast to what John describes in his letter of 1 John. He describes the wonderful fellowship we can have with God. Our very lives can be permeated with the Father and with His Son, Jesus Christ. Wherever we go we can be walking in the light of the Lord.

Since I was a child I have had at some level a desire to be close to God. There were a few moments when the Lord did seem very close. But most of the time it was nothing like fellowship, a shared life with God. So I comforted myself by declaring that our relationship with God is not based on feeling but faith. Still, I hungered for those moments of closeness to Jesus.

Then, I discovered 1 John and realized I had been going at it all wrong.

1 John 1:1-7	When do we have this fellowship with God, with one another? When we walk in the light. What is the light? When are we cleansed from sin? When we walk in the light.
1 John 2:3-11	John has been a follower of Christ for more than sixty years. He is still focused on the commandment they have had from the beginning. When am I living in the light? When am I not living in the light?
John 14:15-23	Jesus is telling how we can experience God the Father and God the Son pitching the tabernacle of their presence over our lives. When does this happen?
1 John 4:7-8	Here John tells us how we can "know" God in a very personal and intimate way.
1 John 4:11-12	When does God live in us? When is His love brought to full expression in and through us?
Isaiah 58:8	When will God's glorious presence surround and protect me? When will God be right there the second I need Him?
Job 29:3-4	Just as in John 14, Job describes having the friendship, the fellowship of God over his tent. Why was God so present?

Psalm 34:15-16   Whom does the Lord watch over? To whom does He respond whenever they need Him?

Psalm 37:23-24   Who gets to hold the right hand of God?

Psalm 11:7   Who will behold God "face to face"?

Magic Seeds

The real shocker came when I discovered that God has every intention of out-giving me. He really is Love.

It does not end when I start to give. In fact, it is only the beginning. Life will flourish in the magic of giving.

Jesus said: "Give, and it will be given to you; good measure, pressed down, shaken together, running over, they will pour into your lap. For whatever measure you deal out to others, it will be dealt to you in return" (Luke 6:38 NASB).

As I start to give, God starts to give me even more. As Jesus said, God's love will pour back into your life so that it will spill right out of the container. You will get an overflow.

God is Love. It is His nature to give. And all He asks is that I also be a giver.

The promises were quite clear. The more I give, the more I receive. God promised that those who are givers will never be in want!

How much will I get? That depends, according to Jesus, on how much I am willing to give. The more I give, the more I will receive. You see, I cannot lose by living out this love commandment!

God is promising to pour His love and blessing into our lives. This does not necessarily mean money, fame, or fantastic health. God will provide His very best for us because He deeply loves us.

So Jesus really did mean it when He declared that He had come to bring us abundant, overflowing life! The trick was that I thought it would come by giving to Him, when in fact it pours into my life when I give to others! That is how the Magic works.

I had truly discovered the things that my heart had longed for on my journey of faith.

In Psalms it says that the one who sows in tears will without a doubt come back rejoicing, bringing the fruits of harvest with him:

Psalm 1	What happens when I delight in doing what the Lord wants? Abundant fruitfulness.
Psalm 37:3-6	We actually can have the desires of our heart!
Psalm 41:1-3	Prosperity and quick recovery are promised to those who are kind to the needy.
Psalm 112	Incredible promises are given to those who are following the New Commandment.
Proverbs 3:9,10	Prosperity is promised to givers.
Proverbs 19:17	The Lord says He owes us one when we are helping His kids.
Isaiah 58:10-12	The true blessing is being a blessing to others. In this chapter we learn how that can and will happen. You can be like an oasis in the desert!
Matthew 10:42	Why is the reward so great? Because of who that little person is!

Luke 6:38	This is a clear indication of our Lord's intention to never be out-given.
John 15:1-16	God's plan is for us to bear abundant fruit. This happens by abiding in Him, which means abiding in His love.
Acts 4:32-34	God's grace upon Christians is linked to their being a loving and giving community.
Acts 10:1-6	God is very aware of the giving even of "non-believers."
2 Corinthians 9:6-11	The amount of our giving is directly related to the size of the harvest. Rule of thumb—start by giving that which will bring you joy as you give. A snowball effect will probably follow. If you wish to be generous, God will always give you stuff to be generous with! The more generous you are, the more stuff you get to give away.
Galatians 6:7-10	The harvest and blessing come in His time, not ours. Sometimes, we may be very discouraged, but we must still take every opportunity to practice the New Commandment.

Philippians
4:15-20

Paul is positive that God will meet all of the Philippians' needs because they have been such wonderful givers.

A Magic Mirror

It will not surprise you to know that I met Cinderella. I have a picture to prove it. It happened at Disney World. And it turned out to be quite a lesson in the Magic of God's love.

As Patty and I were talking to her, she asked us where we were from. When we told her we were from Rochester, New York, she proceeded to tell us, without getting out of character, that she and some of her Disney friends had just visited a camp for children with cancer in that area.

I thought about how incredible it must be to walk into a room of children and bring the presence and wonder of Cinderella with you—the joy, the delight of the children.

Paul tells us that we get to do something even more magical! We get to bring not the mere presence of Cinderella into a room but the presence of Jesus! All of us who have put our faith in Jesus Christ "have had that veil removed so that we can be mirrors that brightly reflect the glory of the Lord. And as the spirit of the Lord works within us, we become more and more like him and reflect his glory even more" (2 Corinthians 3:18 NLT).

What a way to live! Not only can I myself experience the Magic and wonder of God's love, but also as my relationship with Him grows, I can bring His love, His glorious presence into the lives of others.

And so, these are the keys to Magic that came from my efforts to keep my promise to God and myself that day in Florida. It means joining my life with the person of the Magic and wading and floating and swimming in a river of love— life in the Holy Spirit. My prayer is that you will discover

Him and all the Magic He has for you. God is that kind, humble, and gentle carpenter from the village of Nazareth. And life with Him is filled with the wonder and Magic of His love.

Finally, I will challenge you as Len Evans challenged me. Practice the New Commandment for six months with all your heart. Do not worry about being religious; just embrace the privilege of loving the incredible children of God all around you. It will revolutionize your life, and you will know what Jesus meant when He said, "I came that they might have life, and might have it abundantly" (John 10:10b NASB).

Enjoy the Magic of God's love!

Epilogue

I am still living in the Magic and wonder of God's love. I am currently pastor of the little church that welcomed Patty and me with such healing love. It is now called Fairport Community Baptist Church, and I am so grateful to God for the opportunity to serve Him in this way again.

I was reminded of how much my own dream is still alive when I was asked to describe my vision for the church, to be used in a brochure for visitors:

Let me share with you my prayerful hopes and dreams for our church; first, a church where, above anything else, people are treated with unconditional positive regard. In other words, each person is treated as the sacred and special child of God that they truly are. They are valued not for how they perform, not for their success, but simply because they are—"Just As I Am."

Second, a place where people learn about how much they are valued and loved by God, Unconditionally loved! Through the message, the music, the greeting time, the fellowship— just by walking in the door—they will encounter that love by the presence of the Holy Spirit in this place and in us.

My dream, which I strongly believe is from God, is that this will be a place for all of God's (prodigal) children, a place where they will be surrounded by the unconditional love of God and be transformed by it, just as Zaccheus was. I have experienced that love.

I would not have survived without it, and God has clearly called me to treat others in the same way He treated me.

I believe God is going to touch hundreds through such a ministry. Some will come by God's providence, some will come by our loving invitation, some will be touched even though they never enter the physical building. Then, through Bible study, small spiritual-growth groups, informal discipling, and mentoring, we ("prodigals") will learn through God's Word what it means to be members of His household, as in our study of the book of Ephesians. We see in His Word that God has provided to us "everything we need for life and godliness" (2 Peter 1:3 NASB), that He will "meet all your needs according to his glorious riches in Jesus Christ" (Philippians 4:19 NASB), and that we will succeed in God's very best for us. "He who began a good work in you will carry it on to completion" (Philippians 1:6 NASB).

And in all of this we will so love one another that all people will know that we are His disciples.

We sincerely invite you to join us on this wonderful journey with the Lord Jesus Christ.

I would love to hear from you if you have questions about this simple teaching or if you have tried the six-month challenge. You can contact me by calling 585-223-0373 or by email to ptuff@rochester.rr.com.

Printed in the United States
49085LVS00001B/163-219

9 781597 818742